Human Rights

ISSUES

Volume 65

Editor

Craig Donnellan

Independence

Educational Publishers

First published by Independence
PO Box 295
Cambridge CB1 3XP
England

British Library Cataloguing in Publication Data
Human Rights – (Issues Series)
I. Donnellan, Craig II. Series
323

ISBN 1 86168 241 7

Printed in Great Britain
MWL Print Group Ltd

Typeset by
Claire Boyd

Cover
The illustration on the front cover is by
Pumpkin House.

CONTENTS

Introduction

Human Rights is the sixty-fifth volume in the **Issues** series. The aim of this series is to offer up-to-date information about important issues in our world.

Human Rights examines young people's rights and human and civil rights.

The information comes from a wide variety of sources and includes:
Government reports and statistics
Newspaper reports and features
Magazine articles and surveys
Web site material
Literature from lobby groups
and charitable organisations.

It is hoped that, as you read about the many aspects of the issues explored in this book, you will critically evaluate the information presented. It is important that you decide whether you are being presented with facts or opinions. Does the writer give a biased or an unbiased report? If an opinion is being expressed, do you agree with the writer?

Human Rights offers a useful starting-point for those who need convenient access to information about the many issues involved. However, it is only a starting-point. At the back of the book is a list of organisations which you may want to contact for further information.

*****

What's all this about rights?

Information from Save the Children

The United Nations Convention on the Rights of the Child (UNCRC) was drawn up in 1989 and gives children and young people under 18 their own special set of rights.

The UNCRC has 54 'Articles', which are about rights to different things. See below to find out what these rights are. The UNCRC uses the word 'children' to cover everyone under 18.

All young people have rights

- You have the right to be protected from discrimination, whatever your race, sex, colour, religion or anything else.
- When any decisions are made about you, your best interests should be put first.
- All children have the right to life and to grow up.
- You have the right to say what you think, and to have your opinion taken seriously, especially if it's about something that affects you – like your school, family decisions or a court case that involves you.
- You have the right to express yourself freely, and to get the information you need and pass it on, unless this might harm other people.
- You have the right to get useful information from the media, but the government must protect you from any harmful material.
  [Articles 2, 3, 6, 12, 13, 17]

Your personal rights

- You have the right to a name and a nationality. These, and your family background, make up your basic identity. If you lose any of these (maybe because you become

a refugee), you have the right to trace your family and re-establish your nationality.

- You have the right to think and believe what you like, and choose your own religion, but your parents should guide you. You mustn't break the law when saying or doing what you believe.
- You have the right to privacy – like keeping a diary that other people shouldn't read.
- If you are disabled, you have the right to special care and education to help you live a full and independent life.
- If you belong to a minority group (because of your race, religion or language), you have the right to enjoy your own culture, follow your religion and use your own language. You have the right to special protection if you're a

refugee and have been forced to leave your country because of danger.
  [Articles 7, 8, 14, 16, 22, 23, 30]

Your family and home

- Your parents or guardians are responsible for bringing you up, and the government must support them. As you grow up, your parents or guardians should respect your ability to understand, and encourage you to do things for yourself.
- You have the right to live with your parents, if you want to, and to keep in touch with both of them if they separate.
- No one has the right to hurt you. Adults must protect you from violence, abuse or neglect, and if you do get hurt, they must do something about it.
- If you haven't got a family, you have the right to special care – which might mean being adopted, fostered, or living in

another kind of home. If you're adopted, your wishes and needs should be put first – not your parents' or any other adults'. If you're 'in care', you have the right to have your case checked regularly to make sure that you're being treated properly. You have the right to whatever social security benefits the government provides.

- You have the right to enough to eat, adequate clothes, and a roof over your head. If your parents, or whoever looks after you, can't afford these, the government should help them.

[Articles 5, 9, 18, 19, 20, 21, 25, 26, 27]

Your school and work

- You have the right to education and it should be free at primary level.
- If you're punished at school, your dignity must be respected. The aims of education are to develop your personality and talents, prepare you for life as a grown-up, and teach you to respect other people's rights. This includes learning to respect and tolerate different ways of life, different values, and the environment.
- You have the right not to do harmful work. Work should not stop you from learning, being healthy, or growing up. The government must set a minimum age for when children can work, and make sure that you're not working in bad conditions.
- You have the right not to be sexually exploited or abused. No one has the right to do things to your body without your permission. Adults must protect you from prostitution and pornography.
- If you're under 15, you shouldn't have to fight wars or be in an army.

[Articles 28, 29, 32, 34, 38]

Your community and environment

- You have the right to meet other people and join or set up your own groups, as long as this doesn't interfere with other people's rights.

- You have the right to grow up healthy, which means getting proper healthcare and information to help you stay healthy.
- You have the right to play, and to relax by doing things like sport, music, drama and art.
- You have the right to be protected from drugs – you shouldn't be forced to take them, make them, or deal them.
- You have the right not to be tortured, treated cruelly, killed, jailed for life, unlawfully arrested or unlawfully jailed. If you are jailed, you have the right to be kept separate from adults, to see your family, and to get legal help.
- If you break the law, or are accused of doing something wrong, you still have the right to be treated with respect, get legal help, and have a fair hearing.
- You have the right to be protected from war. If you're hurt by war, torture, or any other abuse, you have the right to special care to help you get over it.

[Articles 15, 24, 31, 33, 37, 39, 40]

Why are children and young people's rights important to Save the Children?

Our founder, Eglantyne Jebb, wrote the first children's rights charter in 1923, which later became the UNCRC. So there's nothing new

---

Nearly every country in the world has signed up and agreed to the UN Convention on the Rights of the Child

---

about children's rights – they've been around for nearly a century. And they still underpin everything we do today. The UNCRC is the basis of Save the Children's work, and we try to make sure governments stick to it.

In over 65 countries across the world, Save the Children champions children's rights in its work with:

- families and communities
- children caught up in war
- refugee children
- disabled children
- children in care
- homeless children
- and all other children and young people who suffer hardship, or feel adults are not listening to them.

How does the Convention work?

Nearly every country in the world has signed up and agreed to the UN Convention on the Rights of the Child.

The UNCRC is important because:

- it lists all children's rights in one document
- it makes adults see children as individuals with rights
- it applies to all children and young people everywhere
- it covers the full range of human rights.

It's used to put pressure on governments to ensure children's rights are respected. It has also given children and young people the chance to make their voices heard at the highest level. A United Nations committee measures how well governments who have signed up to it are actually doing. Each government must report back on children's rights in their country. If they're not doing enough, the United Nations makes recommendations about how they can improve.

For more information about Save the Children, please contact: Public Enquiry Unit, Save the Children, 17 Grove Lane, London SE5 8RD. Tel 020 7716 2268, e-mail enquiries@scfuk.org.uk

- The above information is from Save the Children's web site: www.savethechildren.org.uk

© Save the Children

Children lecture MPs on their human rights

By Andrew Sparrow,
Political Correspondent

Six children, aged 10 to 16, became the youngest people ever to give evidence to a committee of MPs and peers.

The politicians are investigating the case for a human rights commission and the witnesses were invited to discuss the advantages of having a children's rights commissioner.

Jean Corston, chairman of the joint committee on human rights, insisted that there was nothing 'tokenist' about her decision to invite the youngsters to appear.

The children spoke for about an hour, reading prepared statements and answering questions, and their performance was praised by the committee.

Fred Tyson Brown, 14, from Wimbourne, Dorset, said that David Blunkett's comment about schools being 'swamped' by young asylum seekers was 'an example of how the Government does not really respect children and young people'.

Scotland, Wales and Northern Ireland have all got or are getting a children's rights commissioner. Fred, who sported shoulder-length hair, said that if England got one, 'he or she would set up offices all over the country where children and young people would be able to drop in and say if they had problems'.

James Sweeney, 16, from Stafford, quoted the UN Convention on the Rights of the Child, which says that children should be told about decisions that affect them.

That did not happen to him when he was being looked after in a care home, he told the committee. He was only consulted about his future when offered the choice between one or two activities, he said.

> *The children spoke for about an hour, reading prepared statements and answering questions, and their performance was praised by the committee*

James also complained about the general lack of support he received. 'Eighty per cent of children in care leave with no qualifications at all. I'm an unproud example of that.'

Andy Butler, 15, from Huddersfield, complained about the media presentation of young people. 'There's a stereotype of young people as thieves. Most of the time it's the older generation who steal.'

Mrs Corston asked Diana Savickaja, 10, from Hackney, east London, to explain what kind of discrimination and human rights problems children faced.

Diana, sitting in a position normally occupied by a minister or a top civil servant, on a seat clearly too big for her, replied quietly, reading from notes. But if the committee thought she would not have much to say, they were wrong.

She mentioned bullying, the plight of Muslim children after September 11 and even the difficulty of trying to claim a child's fare on the bus when you look a bit too old.

The six children were invited to appear because they are all involved with the Children's Rights Alliance for England.

Know your rights

Did you know that you have rights? Did you know that there is a law called the Convention on the Rights of the Child? By Alexander Nurnberg

Your rights are about what you are allowed to do, and what the people responsible for you have to do for you to make sure you are happy, healthy and safe. Of course you also have responsibilities towards other children and adults, to make sure they get their rights. A convention is an agreement between countries to obey the same law. When the government of a country ratifies a convention, that means it agrees to obey the law written down in that convention. Each article of the Convention explains one of your rights.

The Convention on the Rights of the Child is written for lawyers, so it is not easy even for adults to understand. We decided to pick out the rights we think are most important and explain them here in our own words. We have put them into different groups.

You have a right to know what your rights are – it says so in Article 42!

Some of your general rights

These are your general rights protected by the Convention. The other rights are more specific.

Article 1
Everyone under 18 years of age has all the rights in this Convention.

Article 2
You have these rights, whoever you are, whoever your parents are, whatever colour you are, whatever sex or religion you are, whatever language you speak, whether you have a disability, or if you are rich or poor.

Article 3
Whenever an adult has anything to do with you, he or she should do what is best for you.

Article 6
Everyone should recognise that you have the right to live.

United Nations Children's Fund

Article 7
You have the right to have a name, and when you are born, your name, your parents' names and the date should be written down. You have the right to a nationality, and the right to know and be cared for by your parents.

Article 12
Whenever adults make a decision which will affect you in any way, you have the right to give your opinion, and the adults have to take that seriously.

You and your parents
These are the rights which talk about the responsibilities between you and your parents.

Article 9
You should not be separated from your parents unless it is for your own good. For instance, your parents may be hurting you or not taking care of you. Also, if your parents decide to live apart, you will have to live with one or the other of them, but you have the right to contact both parents easily.

Article 10
If you or your parents are living in separate countries, you have the right to get back together and live in the same place.

Article 18
Both of your parents should be involved in bringing you up and they should do what is best for you.

Article 20
If you do not have any parents, or if it is not safe for you to live with your parents, you have the right to special protection and help.

Article 21
If you have to be adopted, adults should make sure that everything is arranged in the way that is best for you.

What you can say and think!
These are the rights which talk about how you can express yourself.

Article 13
You have the right to find out things and say what you think through speaking, writing, making art etc., unless it affects the rights of others.

Article 14
You have the right to think what you like and be whatever religion you want to be. Your parents should help you learn what is right and wrong.

Article 15
You have the right to meet, make friends and make clubs with other people, unless it affects the rights of others.

Article 16
You have the right to a private life. For instance, you can keep a diary that other people are not allowed to see.

Article 17
You have the right to collect information from radios, newspapers, televisions, books etc., from all around the world. Adults should make sure that you get information you can understand.

Article 30
If you come from a minority group, you have the right to enjoy your own culture, practise your own religion and use your own language.

Article 31
You have a right to play.

Keeping you healthy and well
These are the rights which make sure you are healthy, have a good standard of living and can go to school.

Article 23
If you are disabled, either mentally

or physically, you have the right to special care and education to help you grow up in the same way as other children.

Article 24
You have a right to good health. This means that you should have professional care and medicines when you are sick. Adults should try their hardest to make sure that children do not get sick in the first place by feeding and taking good care of them.

Article 27
You have the right to a good enough 'standard of living'. This means that parents have the responsibility to make sure you have food, clothes, a place to live, etc. If parents cannot afford this, the government should help.

Article 28
You have a right to education. You must have primary education, and it must be free. You should also be able to go to secondary school.

Article 29
The purpose of your education is to develop your personality, talents and mental and physical abilities to the fullest. Education should also prepare you to live responsibly and peacefully, in a free society, understanding the rights of other people, and respecting the environment.

Article 32
You have the right to be protected from working in places or conditions that are likely to damage your health or get in the way of your education. If somebody is making money out of your work, you should be paid fairly.

Stopping people hurting you
These are the rights which make sure nobody can hurt you.

Article 11
You should not be kidnapped, and, if you are, the government should try their hardest to get you back.

Article 19
No one should hurt you in any way. Adults should make sure that you are protected from abuse, violence and neglect. Even your parents have no right to hurt you.

Article 22
If you are a refugee (meaning you have to leave your own country because it is not safe for you to live there) you have the right to special protection and help.

Article 33
You have the right to be protected from illegal drugs and from the business of making and selling drugs.

Article 34
You have the right to be protected from sexual abuse. This means that nobody can do anything to your body that you do not want them to do, such as touching you or taking pictures of you or making you say things that you don't want to say.

Article 35
No one is allowed to kidnap or sell you.

Article 37
Even if you do something wrong, no one is allowed to punish you in a way that humiliates you or hurts you badly. You should never be put in prison except as a last resort, and, if you are put in prison, you have the right to special care and regular visits with your family.

Article 38
You have a right to protection in times of war. If you are under fifteen, you should never have to be in an army or take part in a battle.

Article 39
If you have been hurt or neglected in any way, for instance in a war, you have the right to special care and treatment.

Article 40
You have the right to defend yourself if you have been accused of committing a crime. The police and the lawyers and the judges in court should treat you with respect and make sure you understand everything that is going on.

The Convention on the Rights of the Child has 54 articles in all, but most of the rest are about how adults and governments should work together to make sure all children get their rights. You might want to read more about the Convention.

Talk about it with your friends, your parents and your teachers. By telling other people about children's rights, you will be helping other children too. The more people understand that children have rights, the more likely they are to help everyone get what they need to grow up healthy, and safe, and free.

■ The above information is from UNICEF UK's web site which can be found at www.unicef.org.uk
© UNICEF

FAQs about children's rights

The Children's Rights Alliance for England (CRAE) is often asked questions about children's human rights. We have selected 11 of the most 'frequently asked questions', and provided brief answers.

1. What are children's rights?
Children's rights are a set of entitlements for all children, of whatever age and background. Most children's rights supporters use the UN Convention on the Rights of the Child (UNCRC) as their guide to children's rights. This is a comprehensive international treaty that took 10 years to develop. The UNCRC grants children in all parts of the world a comprehensive set of social, political and civil rights, designed to take into account their vulnerability, particular needs and 'evolving capacity'.

Some people often mistakenly believe that children's rights are all about children and young people acting irresponsibly with no thought for others. Another common misconception is that children's rights deprive children of their childhood. Human rights treaties, including the UNCRC, never give human beings unfettered rights: children, like adults, must respect the rights of others. In addition, there is no need to be concerned about children being robbed of their childhood: the UNCRC was designed completely around children's lives and needs and includes, for example, the right to play and the right to education.

2. What are the basic beliefs behind children's rights?
Children's rights supporters believe that children's and young people's lives are important and valid NOW. We do not think that children's worth rests on the fact that they will one day become adults. We also accept that children and young people are widely discriminated against as a group, and we are committed to working with them to make real improvements in their lives

---

Children's rights supporters believe that children's and young people's lives are important and valid NOW

---

and status. Finally, supporters of children's rights strongly believe that children and young people should always have a say when decisions are being made that affect their lives, either as individuals or as a group. Sometimes it will be necessary for children and young people to have support from independent people to help them express their views and ideas.

3. Can children have rights without responsibilities?
Children and young people do have responsibilities: many have jobs, some care for relatives, a large proportion are school or college students, and they all must respect other people's rights and act within the law. However, these are not connected to their human rights, which everybody has from the moment they're born.

4. How old do children have to be before their views must be listened to?
The UN Convention on the Rights of the Child (UNCRC), which has

the status of international law, does not give a minimum age for when children must be listened to. Article 12 of the UNCRC states that 'any child who is capable of forming his or her views [has] the right to express those views freely'. Research shows that very young children can form views on extremely complex matters such as medical care and treatment.

5. Can children go to court if their rights are ignored?

Children and young people are not able to go to court if their rights under the UN Convention on the Rights of the Child are ignored. However, children and young people can use the courts if their rights under law made in the UK are ignored. This includes rights contained in the Human Rights Act, the Children Act 1989, sex, race and disability equality laws and education legislation for example.

6. Isn't there a risk that emphasising rights will encourage children to disrespect adults?

Promoting children's and young people's human rights encourages mutual respect and positive behaviour. A commitment to children's human rights shows that adults respect children and young people, and take them seriously as individual people. This can only make relationships better, not worse.

7. Isn't it better to talk about children's needs rather than children's rights?

Children's human rights are based on their needs. An emphasis on rights rather than needs shows a commitment to seeing and respecting

children and young people as citizens who have justified claims on society.

Children's rights treaties always make clear that parents have the first responsibility to meet children's needs, but that if parents cannot meet their responsibilities then society and the state must shoulder them. All political creeds and parties recognise that children have the right to have their needs met.

Definitions of what children need are subject to professional and political judgement, yet children's human rights – as expressed by the UN Convention on the Rights of the Child (UNCRC) – are clear and universal: they apply to all children. It took 10 years for the United Nations to prepare the UNCRC as a comprehensive statement on what children across the globe require to achieve their full potential as people.

8. What happens when children's rights clash with cultural or religious traditions?

The UN Convention on the Rights of the Child (UNCRC) stresses the role of parents in looking after, guiding and supporting children, according to children's 'evolving capacities'. This means that as soon as children are able to make informed judgements about cultural and religious traditions, they have the right to exercise choice.

Some aspects of cultural or religious traditions have a lasting impact on children and young people – genital mutilation for example. In these circumstances, decisions should never be taken until children and young people are able to exercise an informed and free choice.

9. Compared to other European countries, how well does UK law respect children's rights?

The UK locks up more young people than any other European country; one in three children is living in poverty; child asylum seekers are neglected and degraded; and school students outside of Scotland are not given any legal rights to participate in key decisions, including when they are excluded. UK law still allows

parents to hit children, based on an 1860 court case where a judge said hitting children was acceptable so long as it was 'reasonable'. In 10 other European countries independent watchdogs have been set up to promote and safeguard children's human rights: progress in the UK in this area has been painfully slow, although there are positive developments in Wales.

10. Is there an age limit for when children and young people can instruct solicitors?

There is no lower age limit for children instructing solicitors but they have to demonstrate that they understand the processes involved. In criminal matters, children are seen to be competent to instruct solicitors from the age of 10 years.

11. Is there anyone in the Government who has a special responsibility to promote and respect children's human rights?

The Children and Young People's Unit has a special responsibility to prepare reports for the Committee on the Rights on the Child on how well the UK is implementing the UN Convention on the Rights of the Child (UNCRC). The Minister of State for Health, Alan Milburn MP, is the person within the Government who therefore has most responsibility for the UNCRC. However, a new Minister for Young People has now been appointed – John Denham MP – who may have a special responsibility to ensure children's human rights are respected.

■ The above information is from the Children's Rights Alliance for England's (CRAE) web site which can be found at www.crights.org.uk

© The Children's Rights Alliance for England (CRAE)

Birthrights

British public back change in law to give children a right to their identity

A poll commissioned by the Children's Society puts added pressure on the Government to end discrimination against children born through donor-assisted conception.

The MORI poll – the first ever to reveal the public's attitude on the issue of anonymity for sperm and egg donors – shows that the British public overwhelmingly support the rights of donor-conceived children to have a statutory right to know the identity of their biological parents. It found that:

■ 80 per cent of those surveyed believe donor-conceived children should have a statutory right at 18 to know the genetic history of their biological parents.

■ by contrast, only 19 per cent believe parents should be given the right to have donor-conceived children without telling them who their birth parents are.

■ 69 per cent of people feel that withholding information about a child's biological parents promotes secrecy and believe parents should be encouraged to be more open with their children.

■ 83 per cent of people believe that children over 18 should have access to their biological parents' health and medical history.

The results come as the Government considers changes to the Human Fertilisation and Embryology Authority Act 1990 to allow donor-conceived people greater access to identifying information about donors.

The six-month Department of Health consultation is due to end on 1 July 2002, but any changes will not be retrospective.

'Children have been living under the shadow of legislation that has denied them the right to the most basic information about themselves for too long,' says Julia Feast, Project Manager at the Children's Society. 'The results from this poll are too powerful for the Government to ignore.

'Current legislation puts the right of a parent to have a child before the needs of children to have essential information about their genetic history and this imbalance must change.

'It's time for the Government to acknowledge that openness and honesty should now become the accepted practice, so that all of tomorrow's children grow up with dignity and a right to their identity.'

Under existing laws, donor-conceived children have no right to information about their genetic parents – only the right, at 16, to be told whether someone they intend to marry is genetically related them and at 18, if they were conceived by egg or sperm donation.

Around 1,500 people are born through donor-assisted conception each year and are the only people who are legally denied the right to access information about their origins.

David Gollancz, a lawyer and father of two children, was 12 when he found out in 1965 that he had been conceived by donor insemination. He believes the law should give priority to people's right to know the truth about their identity.

'No one has the right to deliberately deceive people, or deprive them of information about their personal history. But the state has allowed this to be done to a whole generation.

Survey	Strongly agree	Tend to agree	Neither agree nor disagree	Tend to dis-agree	Strongly disagree	Agree	Dis-agree	Don't know
1. Once they have reached 18, all children should have the right to know the genetic history of biological parents	40%	41%	8%	4%	2%	80%	7%	5%
2. All parents should have a right to have children without telling them the genetic history of their biological parents	4%	15%	18%	32%	25%	19%	56%	7%
3. Parents should be given a choice as to whether or not a child aged 18 or over has the right to information about their genetic history	10%	25%	12%	27%	19%	35%	46%	7%
4. Donor-assisted conception should only be offered if offspring are given the right to information about their genetic history when they reach 18	23%	39%	15%	10%	5%	62%	15%	8%
5. Donors should have the right to withhold information about their genetic history when they donate eggs or sperm to help other couples conceive	8%	16%	11%	25%	33%	24%	59%	7 %
6. Children aged 18 or over should have the right to information about their parents' health and medical background that could affect them (e.g. genetically inherited diseases or a genetic predisposition towards a disease)	46%	37%	7%	3%	2%	83%	5%	5%
7. Children from donor-assisted conception should have the same rights as adopted children to know who their biological parents are if they want to	34%	36%	11%	9%	4%	69%	13%	7%
8. There is too much secrecy about donor-assisted conception and we should encourage parents to be more open about it	25%	43%	18%	5%	2%	68%	7%	7%

The survey was conducted on a sample of 1,033 adults aged 15+ in 188 sampling points across Great Britain between 23 and 28 May 2002.
* indicates a value of less than half of one per cent but greater than zero.

Source: The Children's Society

'I am delighted that this poll has shown that the public understands this and the Government must now change the law and protect children's rights.'

Currently, fertility clinics only collect and pass on details about a donor's genetic medical condition to parents of donor-conceived children. This means, for example, that doctors treating donor-conceived children are relying on a limited, and sometimes incorrect, medical history.

In February 2002 this year, a Dutch man who was the biological father of 18 donor-conceived children, was found to be suffering from a hereditary, degenerative brain disorder. After three years, the fertility clinic finally decided that the parents of these children needed to be told, as they have a 50 per cent chance of developing the disease.

Based on interviews with over 1,000 people throughout Britain, the poll also reveals that donor-conceived people in Britain should have the same rights to information as adopted people:

- two-thirds support changes in the law to give people from donor-assisted conception the same rights as adopted people, who, at 18, are entitled to a copy of their birth certificate, showing identifying information about their birth parents.

Research by the Children's Society shows how important it is to allow adopted people the right to identifying information about their genetic history. It shows that over 80 per cent of adopted people who search for their birth relatives, have done so to satisfy a long-standing curiosity about their origins and 80 per cent said that important questions about their identity had been answered after receiving information about their birth parents.

The Children's Society has the reputation of being one of the most innovative children's charities in the UK. We work with some of the country's most vulnerable children and young people, including young runaways living in danger on the streets, teenagers on remand in prison, and children – some still at primary school – who face exclusion or bullying. We aim to be a positive force for change wherever unnecessary suffering and injustice damage young lives.

- The above information is from the Children's Society's web site: www.childrenssociety.org.uk

© The Children's Society

Right Here Right Now

The case for a children's rights commissioner for England

Introduction

Right Here Right Now is a group of children and young people campaigning for a Children's Rights Commissioner for England, funded from 2001 to 2002 by NSPCC. Since July 2001, when the Children's Rights Alliance for England (CRAE) recruited over 20 children and young people from across the country, we have designed a postcard and website, spoken at conferences, and met with MPs and Children's Rights Commissioners from other countries.

Three members of the group made history in June 2002 – when we gave oral evidence in Parliament to the Joint Committee on Human Rights. One member of the group also gave written evidence on why children and young people living in England need a Children's Rights Commissioner.

Right Here Right Now has produced this information for children and young people to let you know about the campaign to get a Children's Rights Commissioner for England as soon as possible, and so that many more of you can join us in

Written by Andy Butler and Laura Dent, with Jay Sweeney, Right Here Right Now

the campaign. At the same time CRAE has published a more detailed booklet with the same title.

What is the UN Convention on the Rights of the Child?

In 1991 the United Kingdom (UK) Government ratified the United Nations Convention on the Rights of the Child. Every government in the world apart from the USA and Somalia has ratified the Convention. This means they have agreed to make sure that all the country's laws and policies follow what the Convention says about children's human rights. The Convention gives everyone under 18 a complete set of rights and freedoms, setting out the way they should be treated, justly and fairly, and how they should be able to grow up in an atmosphere of happiness, love and understanding.

Some of the Convention's most important rules are that governments should make laws and special arrangements so that:

- all children can have all the rights in the Convention (Article 4)
- all adults and all children know about the Convention (Article 42)
- everyone can know what the Government says in its reports to the Committee on the Rights of the Child, which works at the United Nations in Geneva, Switzerland (Article 44.6).

The best way for governments to show they take children's rights seriously is to set up a champion for children (everyone under 18) – someone independent of the Government to fight for all the rights of all children. In October 2002 the Committee on the Rights of the Child in Geneva told the UK Government that it should set up powerful independent human rights bodies (children's rights commissioners) for children all across the country, and that children should have a big say in how they are set up and what they do.

What is a Commissioner?

Children's Rights Commissioners are national watchdogs for children and young people. They are not part of the Government. They monitor, protect and promote all the rights of the Convention for children. Commissioners must:

- Have enough power to check how children in this country are treated, and get things changed;
- Try to make sure everyone understands and respects children's rights;
- Check that these rights are being taken seriously and made real in the country's laws and policies;
- Point out to the Government what effect new laws may have on children's rights, and where existing laws need changing;
- Make sure children's complaints are properly heard and dealt with, and that they can get support when they need to complain;
- Look into and investigate some aspects of children's rights, and let the public know about important examples of individual complaints;
- Stand up for children's rights and interests in some court cases.

Why England needs a Commissioner

The Government has shown it is serious about human rights. It has brought in the Human Rights Act 1998, and set up the Children and Young People's Unit and a Minister for Children and Young People. The Human Rights Act protects some children's rights, but not as many as the Convention, and it is not easy for children to use it. The Children and Young People's Unit and the Minister are part of the Government, so they cannot be independent.

The Children's Commissioner for Wales was set up two years ago, and children in Scotland and Northern Ireland will soon have their own commissioners. Now the Committee on the Rights of the Child has reminded the Government that all the UK's children should have a commissioner, and that includes the 11.3 million of us in England.

A Commissioner could help make England a more children's rights friendly country, making sure that children and young people are respected and not ignored, that they

are heard and taken seriously. Article 12 of the Convention states that all children have the right to express their views freely about everything that affects them, and to have their views taken seriously.

A Commissioner – by highlighting the problems and proposing solutions – could help end poverty, reduce child abuse and improve children's lives in many ways.

Without a Children's Rights Commissioner children and young people's rights will not be fully respected, and young people will not always be asked for their views and opinions. We need a powerful link between children and young people and the Government. A Children's Rights Commissioner would make that link.

What you could do

We need all children and young people to get involved with our campaign. You can do this by joining Right Here Right Now or by writing a letter to your local MP or the Prime Minister to say why England should have a Children's Rights Commissioner. Below is a letter you could copy and send with your own ideas. To find out who your MP is, have a look at the website listed below.

Web links

Right Here Right Now – www.rhrn.org.uk
CRAE – www.crights.org.uk
Children's Commissioner for Wales – www.childcom.org.uk
Children and Young People's Unit – www.cypu.gov.uk
List of MPs – www.parliament.uk/directories/directories.cfm
NSPCC – www.nspcc.org.uk
UN Convention – www.unhchr.ch/html/menu3/b/k2crc.htm

Contacting us

Write to us: Right Here Right Now, c/o CRAE, 94 White Lion Street, London, N1 9PF. Phone: 0207 278 8222. Email: info@rhrn.org.uk

© *Children's Rights Alliance for England (CRAE)*

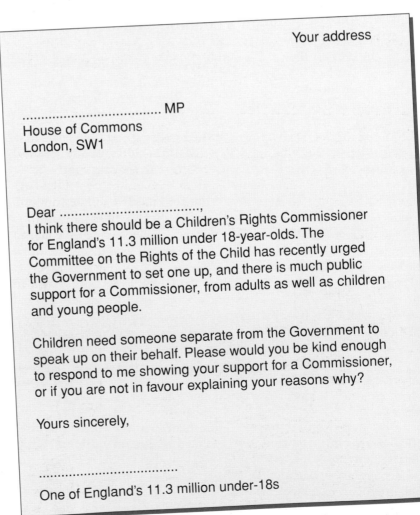

Your address

.... MP
House of Commons
London, SW1

Dear ....,
I think there should be a Children's Rights Commissioner for England's 11.3 million under 18-year-olds. The Committee on the Rights of the Child has recently urged the Government to set one up, and there is much public support for a Commissioner, from adults as well as children and young people.

Children need someone separate from the Government to speak up on their behalf. Please would you be kind enough to respond to me showing your support for a Commissioner, or if you are not in favour explaining your reasons why?

Yours sincerely,

....
One of England's 11.3 million under-18s

Parental responsibility and children's rights

Introduction

Parental responsibility (PR) describes the legal relationship between parents – and in certain circumstances other adults – and their child(ren). PR normally lasts until the child is 18. It is not defined in the Children Act and contains no requirement to promote the child's welfare or to consult the child in decision-making. The way adults exercise their PR should reflect the evolving capacities, and age and maturity of the child. There are a range of laws which give children rights at different ages. In practice, young people at 16 are relatively independent.

The Children Act 1989 does not require parents or others with parental responsibility to consult their children or to take their views into account in making decisions about their upbringing. However, in

---

Other people in charge of children, such as childminders, teachers or foster carers, do not have parental responsibility

---

1985 the House of Lords said that parental powers to control their children dwindle as the child matures. The rights of parents should give way to the child's right to make decisions when 'he or she is of sufficient understanding and intelligence' to be able to make up his or her own mind. This is known as the Gillick principle. This notion of children's rights to respect for their evolving capacities in parental decision making is also reflected in Article 5 of the UNCRC .

Other people in charge of children, such as childminders, teachers or foster carers, do not have parental responsibility. However, they do have a duty of care to behave as a reasonable parent would do to ensure the child's safety. This is sometimes called 'in loco parentis'. In an emergency they can take reasonable steps to promote the child's welfare.

Parents, unmarried fathers and others

Mothers and married fathers – who are married to the mother of their children – automatically have parental responsibility – PR – and this continues even if they divorce. Unmarried fathers can obtain parental responsibility by going to

court for a parental responsibility order or by entering into a formal parental responsibility agreement with the mother. The Adoption and Children Bill presently going through Parliament provides that unmarried fathers registered on the child's birth certificate will automatically get PR.

Other people may acquire parental responsibility, for example, where a residence order – specifying with whom the child is to live – is made by the court or on the appointment of a guardian where a parent has died. The local authority obtains PR when a care order is made by a court.

There are a range of laws which give children rights at different ages. In practice, young people at 16 are relatively independent

---

The Adoption and Children Bill proposes that stepparents can enter into parental responsibility agreements with their spouse and other parent or apply to the court for a parental responsibility order.

Each person with PR can act independently of the other. There is no requirement in law to consult with the other person unless this breaches the law, such as taking the child out of the country, or it is against a court order. If there are disagreements about PR the court can make a prohibited steps order – stopping a parent from doing something – or a specific issues order – telling the parent(s) to do something in a certain way.

Key areas of parental responsibility

Names
Mothers, married fathers and others with parental responsibility have the right to choose the name of their child. However, the courts have said that in any dispute about name change an application should be made to the court irrespective of the parent's legal status.

Gillick: competent young people should be able to change their name without their parents' consent but they may need to apply to court for permission to seek a specific issue order.

Religion
Gillick: competent young people should be able to choose their own religion or no religion. If there is a dispute between the parents and/or the child, the court can be involved. In a domestic case the court considered Article 9 of the European Convention – freedom of thought, conscience and religion – in relation to the circumcision of a five-year-

old child. The judge concluded that where both parents have equal rights under Article 9, limitations on one parent's rights can be imposed if these conflict with the rights of the other parent and the child and are not in the best interests of the child.

Medical treatment
At 16, young people have the right to give consent to medical, dental and surgical treatment. This includes contraceptive advice and treatment. Young people under the age of 16 can give consent provided that the doctor or health worker thinks the young person is mature enough to understand what is involved in the treatment and the consequences of this. The law says that doctors should encourage young people to inform their parents, however, they may give treatment without parental knowledge or consent if the young person does not wish to involve them. These principles also apply to termination of pregnancy but in practice doctors very rarely perform abortions for under-16s without parental consent because of the possible risks associated with general anaesthesia.

Young people under the age of 18 do not have an absolute right to refuse consent to medical treatment. Refusal to give consent in cases concerning serious mental health or life-threatening situations can be overridden if their parents – or if they are in care, the local authority – disagree with their decision. This should require a court hearing and the courts have said that the child's views are an important matter in its determination. It is unlikely that this position will be changed by the Human Rights Act. Cases decided by the European Court have held that lack of consent for treatment, such as force feeding, necessary to prevent death or serious injury would not be treated as degrading or inhuman treatment in accordance with Article 3 of the Convention on Human Rights.

Corporal punishment
Parents have the right to administer reasonable physical chastisement to their children. This

is a defence in law to a charge of assault. The law has banned corporal punishment in schools and for children in foster and residential care. In a unanimous decision the European Court found a breach of Article 3 – degrading and inhuman treatment – against the British Government in a case where a boy had been beaten with a garden cane by his stepfather. The Government is unwilling to abolish the defence of reasonable physical chastisement and is consulting on a range of alternative options to comply with this judgement.

Leaving home
In law, under-16s cannot leave home unless their parents agree. Alternatively a court may make a residence order to another person such as a relative or an adult friend. This can be done on the application of the adult concerned, or by the child provided that the court has first decided that the child has sufficient understanding to make the application.

In law, under-16s cannot leave home unless their parents agree. Alternatively a court may make a residence order to another person such as a relative or an adult friend

---

The police will return young runaways under 16 to their parents – or their care authority, if in care – unless they have reasonable cause to believe that the child is at risk. In these circumstances the police may hold the child in police protection. The police will liaise with social services, which may take further action for the child's protection. The police are unlikely to return over-16s to their parents.

■ The above information is from Liberty's 'Your Rights' web site which can be found at www.yourrights.org.uk

© Liberty

Physical punishment in the home

NSPCC call for government rethink on hitting children following UN report

Inadequate legal protection from physical punishment in the home is expected to be one of the main concerns of a United Nations report to be published on Friday 4 October 2002.

The UN Committee on the Rights of the Child will list the areas where the Government is out of step with the spirit of the Convention on the Rights of the Child, which the UK ratified in 1991.

In its last report, in 1995, the UN Committee criticised the UK law of 'reasonable chastisement', stating that it 'does not appear to be compatible with the provisions and principles of the UN Convention'.

The NSPCC believes that the 1860 law of 'reasonable chastisement' allows some parents to hit their children harshly and frequently with impunity and sends out a dangerous message to all parents that it is acceptable to hit their children.

In 1998, the European Court of Human Rights ruled that UK law does not protect children adequately. However, last November the Department of Health decided not to change the law in England and Wales against the advice of child protection professionals.

NSPCC Director Mary Marsh said: 'Hitting children is incompatible with the UN Convention on the Rights of the Child. The UN's report will add to the growing pressure on the Government to rethink its inaction over protecting children from being hit.'

The most recent country to ban physical punishment was Germany in 2000 and the first was Sweden in 1979

The NSPCC and the 350 organisations in the Children Are Unbeatable Alliance want the law changed to give children the same protection from being hit as adults – no more, no less. Such a change in the law should go hand in hand with mass public education about positive and more effective ways of bringing up children, including extensive provision of parenting support programmes.

A MORI survey for the NSPCC in February 2002 found that, provided parents were not prosecuted for 'trivial smacks', a majority (58 per cent) of people in England and Wales support changing the law to give children protection from being hit.

Notes

Article 19 of the UN Convention on the Rights of the Child states that Governments should 'take all appropriate legislative, administrative, social and educational measures to protect the child from all forms of physical or mental violence, injury or abuse, neglect of negligent treatment, maltreatment or exploitation, including sexual abuse, while in the care of parent, legal guardian or any other person who has the care of the child'.

Children are protected from being hit by law in Germany, Finland, Sweden, Denmark, Austria, Norway, Croatia, Cyprus, Latvia and Israel. The most recent country to ban physical punishment was Germany in 2000 and the first was Sweden in 1979.

Seven in ten social workers say that 'the existence of "reasonable chastisement" in law sends a message to abusive and potentially abusive parents that persistent and harsh physical punishment is acceptable' (survey of NSPCC child protection professionals, December 2001).

A majority of parents (57 per cent) say that physical punishment is the wrong way to discipline children. More than three-quarters of parents who have used physical punishment (79 per cent) feel upset afterwards.

(MORI for the NSPCC, May 2002.)

■ The above information is from NSPCC's web site which can be found at www.nspcc.org.uk

© NSPCC 2002

Children are unbeatable!

An outline of Barnardo's campaign

The facts

- Children are the only people who do not have legal protection against all levels of violence.
- Physical punishment can lead to more serious injuries and to child abuse.
- Physical punishment is not effective in changing a child's behaviour and sets children the wrong example.
- Studies show that over 90% of children have been smacked, spanked or beaten.

Physical punishment can be dangerous. Smacking is more likely to be a result of frustration or stress rather than a planned action, which increases the risk of violence escalating, leading to more serious injuries such as brain damage. Studies show that physical punishment has a strong tendency to escalate. Many cases of child abuse begin with punishment that got out of hand.

There is no evidence that physical punishment has any effect in changing a child's behaviour and [that it] sets children a bad example. Parents who use it are teaching their children that physical force is an acceptable way to resolve problems. Many studies show that children who are physically punished are more likely to develop aggressive attitudes, get involved in bullying at school and in aggressive behaviour and crime as they grow up.

The law

It is a criminal offence for an adult to hit another adult, but if a parent hits a child as a punishment, they can claim it was 'reasonable chastisement'. This is a common law freedom which is centuries old, and has been interpreted in the courts to include the use of belts and other implements.

Article 19 of the UN Convention on the Rights of the Child upholds children's right to be protected from 'all forms of physical or mental violence'. The UN committee insists that continued legal and social acceptance of physical punishment is not compatible with full implementation of the convention and has called upon the British government to change the law and undertake a public awareness campaign as part of fulfilling its obligations as a signatory to the convention.

Sweden, Finland, Denmark, Norway, Austria, Cyprus, Croatia and Latvia have all banished the physical punishment of children, and progress is being made towards this goal in Italy, Bulgaria, Germany, Belgium, Ireland and Israel. The effect of legal reform has been to change attitudes to children and reduce violence.

- The above information is from Barnardo's web site which can be found at www.barnardos.org.uk

© Barnardo's 2002

What is Barnardo's doing?

Barnardo's believes that

- All children should have the same protection as adults under the law on assault.
- A change in law should be supported by an ongoing programme of public education promoting non-violent, positive forms of discipline.
- Only a full ban on all forms of physical punishment for children will send the message that hitting children is unacceptable and encourage the use of non-violent forms of discipline.

Barnardo's has been a member of the EPOCH (End Physical Punishment of Children) campaign since 1995 and in 1999 was part of the strategy group for a new alliance: Children Are Unbeatable! The alliance now has 260 organisations and many prominent individuals signed up to its aims.

As one of the largest children's charities in the UK, Barnardo's confronts the issue of physical punishment through many strands of its work, including support to families, parent education, child protection work, work with families affected by domestic violence, and foster and adoptive care.

Physical punishment is banned in all Barnardo's projects, and the use of positive parenting methods is actively encouraged. Our experience shows that where physical punishment is forbidden, the adults involved can quickly adapt to alternatives and see the benefits. Foster carers who may initially be sceptical that non-violent and positive forms of discipline can be effective will often report that not only is it effective and that it is a better framework for children, but that as a result of learning these methods they have been able to move away from the use of physical punishment with their own children.

Barnardo's works with mothers and fathers to improve their parenting skills and help develop relationships with their children. Many of the charity's family centres provide support and practical advice for parents who may themselves have experienced physical abuse as children, and whose financial and social circumstances may undermine their ability to cope with their children.

Barnardo's has produced two booklets, in partnership with the Early Years Network and supported by charitable and financial services group IOF Foresters. *Getting Positive About Discipline* aims to help parents to deal with common discipline problems without resorting to smacking or humiliating their children. *Why Speak Out Against Smacking?* explains why legal change is necessary and deals with the common myths engendered by the 'smacking debate'. Both documents are available from Barnardo's publications on 01268 520224 priced £1.

Children's rights

Information from Human Rights Watch

Children around the world suffer appalling abuses. Too often, street children are killed or tortured by police. Children as young as seven or eight are recruited or kidnapped to serve as soldiers in military forces. Sometimes as young as six years old, children are forced to work under extremely difficult conditions, often as bonded labourers or in forced prostitution. They are imprisoned in inhumane conditions, sometimes in cells with adults. They are often brutalised by guards or not protected from assaults by other inmates. Refugee children, often separated from their families, are vulnerable to exploitation, sexual abuse, or domestic violence. Ironically, within the care of the state, children are often subject to abuse and mistreatment – orphaned and abandoned children are housed in appalling institutions where they suffer from cruelty and neglect; many die. For many students, life in and outside of the classroom is intolerable – at the hands of peers and teachers, many children suffer under acts of discrimination, abuse, sexual violence, and harassment. In many countries, teachers are allowed to use corporal punishment on children. Children are discriminated against in education because of their race or ethnicity. Children orphaned or otherwise affected by HIV/AIDS are discriminated against and often are left to fend for themselves.

> *Sometimes as young as six years old, children are forced to work under extremely difficult conditions, often as bonded labourers or in forced prostitution*

In the past, this huge and largely voiceless population has fallen through the cracks in the international human rights arena. Traditional children's humanitarian groups have focused mainly on vital survival and development projects, and have rarely addressed other human rights concerns because they could not afford to antagonise host governments. Human rights groups have focused chiefly on the rights of adults. As the human rights movement was founded out of concern for political dissidents, it has sometimes overlooked those – like children – whose persecution is unrelated to their political views.

The Convention on the Rights of the Child put children's rights on the world's agenda; it is the most widely ratified treaty in the world. Adopted by the United Nations General Assembly on 20 November, 1989, the Convention promises children around the world the right to life, liberty, education, and health care. It provides protection to children in armed conflict, protection from discrimination, protection from torture or cruel, inhuman or degrading treatment or punishment, protection within the justice system, and protection from economic exploitation, in addition to many other fundamental protections. Despite the convention's near-universal ratification (only the US and Somalia have not ratified it), children are still denied their basic rights.

■ The above information is from Human Rights Watch's web site which can be found at www.hrw.org

Child labour remains 'massive problem'

Information from the International Labour Organization (ILO)

Ten years after launching a world-wide campaign against child labour, the International Labour Office (ILO) has launched a comprehensive new look at the problem. The findings are cause for concern; despite 'significant progress' in efforts to abolish child labour, the report says an alarming number of children remain trapped in its worst forms. These and other issues will top the discussion at the International Labour Conference in June as well as the launch of the first World Day Against Child Labour.

A *Future Without Child Labour*,[1] the ILO's most comprehensive study on the subject to date, notes that there has been a worldwide response to calls for abolishing child labour, especially in its worst forms, through direct action at the local, national and international levels. However, child labour remains a problem on a massive scale, according to Director-General Juan Somavia, who is calling for a redoubling of efforts to fight the practice.

Among the key findings:
- One in every six children aged 5 to 17 – or 246 million children – are involved in child labour.
- One in every eight children in the world – some 179 million children aged 5 to 17 – is still exposed to the worst forms of child labour, which endanger their physical, mental or moral well-being.
- About 111 million in hazardous work are under 15, and should be 'immediately withdrawn from this work'.
- An additional 59 million youths aged 15 to 17 should receive urgent and immediate protection from hazards at work, or be withdrawn from such work.
- Some 8.4 million children are caught in 'unconditional' worst forms of child labour, including slavery, trafficking, debt bondage and other forms of forced labour, forced recruitment for armed conflict, prostitution, pornography, and other illicit activities.
- Child labour continues to be a global phenomenon – no country or region is immune, the report says. A wide range of crises – including natural disasters, sharp economic downturns, the HIV/AIDS pandemic, and armed conflicts – increasingly draw the young into debilitating child labour, including illegal and clandestine forms such as prostitution, drug trafficking, pornography, and other illicit activities.

The report was produced as part of the follow-up to the 1998 ILO Declaration on Fundamental Principles and Rights at Work. The Declaration reaffirmed the commitment of all ILO member States to respect, promote, and realize the rights of workers and employers to freedom of association and collective bargaining, and to be free from forced or compulsory labour, child labour, and discrimination.

Has the number of child labourers increased or decreased? The figures in the new report differ from the previously accepted estimate of some 250 million working children aged 5 to 14 in developing countries – the best estimate possible in 1996, when it was first produced. The report notes that the latest methods of gathering data provide a more precise picture of the problem of child labour, its distribution among regions and between age groups, and therefore provide figures that are not open to simple comparison with the original estimate.

The shape of the problem

The report describes child labour at the start of the twenty-first century as 'endlessly varied and infinitely volatile'. Drawing on recent survey data, it says an estimated 352 million children aged 5 to 17 are currently engaged in economic activity of some kind.

Of these, some 106 million are engaged in types of work acceptable for children who have reached the minimum age for employment (usually 15 years) or in light work, such as household chores or work undertaken as part of a child's education [see ILO Minimum Age Convention, 1973 (No. 138)].

The remaining 246 million children are involved in child labour which the ILO says should be abolished. These forms include:
- Work performed by a child under the minimum age specified for a particular kind of work by national legislation or international standards.
- Hazardous work which jeopardises the physical, mental, or moral well-being of a child, either because of its nature or the conditions in which it is performed.
- 'Unconditional' worst forms of child labour as defined in the ILO Worst Forms of Child Labour Convention, 1999 (No. 182).[2]

In terms of geographical distribution, the Asia-Pacific region harbours the largest absolute number of working children between the ages of 5 and 14, with some 127 million, or 60 per cent of the world total. Sub-Saharan Africa is second with 48 million, or 23 per cent of the total, followed by Latin America and the Caribbean with 17.4 million, or 8 per cent, and the Middle East and North Africa with 13.4 million, or 6 per cent.

The report says about 2.5 million, or 1 per cent of the world's child labourers, are in the industrialised countries, while another 2.4 million are found in transition economies.

Surveys in developing countries indicate that the vast majority (70 per cent) of children who work are engaged in such primary sectors as agriculture, fishing, hunting and forestry. Some 8 per cent are involved in manufacturing, wholesale and retail trade, restaurants and hotels; 7 per cent in domestic work and services; 4 per cent in transport, storage, and communication; and 3 per cent in construction, mining, and quarrying.

Child labour often assumes serious proportions in commercial agriculture associated with global markets for cocoa, coffee, cotton, rubber, sisal, tea, and other commodities. Studies in Brazil, Kenya, and Mexico have shown that children under 15 make up between 25 and 30 per cent of the total labour force in the production of various commodities. The report notes that 'in many developed countries, agriculture is also the sector in which most children work', and that 'family farms are a common exemption from minimum age legislation'.

The informal economy, in which workers are not recognised or protected under the legal and regulatory frameworks of the labour market, is where the most child labourers are found by far.

'The preponderance of child labour in the informal economy, beyond the reach of most formal institutions in countries at all levels of income, represents one of the principal challenges to its effective abolition,' says the report.

Some work, such as mining and deep-sea fishing, is obviously dangerous, while other work, which at first sight may appear harmless, may be similarly hazardous, especially for young, undernourished, and otherwise vulnerable children.

Causes and solutions

The report lists the many causes of child labour, all of which must be addressed. While poverty is a major factor, there are many other related causes, such as economic and political instability, discrimination,

migration, criminal exploitation, traditional cultural practices, a lack of decent work for adults, inadequate social protection, a lack of schools, and the desire for consumer goods.

On the demand side, factors include a lack of law enforcement, the desire on the part of some employers for a cheap and flexible workforce, and the low profitability and productivity of small-scale family enterprises which cannot afford adult paid labour.

In spite of the difficulty of addressing all of these causes, the ILO report insists that 'the campaign for universal ratification of Convention No. 182 has given the general fight against child labour a new urgency and scope, by focusing world attention on its worst forms'. Since its unanimous adoption by the International Labour Conference in 1999, Convention No. 182 has been ratified by nearly 120 of the ILO's 175 member States. In addition, the ILO Minimum Age Convention, 1973 (No. 138), has been ratified by 116 member States as of 25 April.

'The world is increasingly aware of child labour, and demanding action to stop it,' Mr Somavia said. 'A majority of governments across the world now acknowledge the existence of the problem – on greater or smaller scales and in different forms. Many have already set out to measure and understand it, and are taking action against it.'

The report will be discussed at the ILO's 90th International Labour Conference, on 12 June in Geneva by the organisation's tripartite partners. On that day, the ILO is also launching an International Day Against Child Labour. The purpose of this initiative is to strengthen the international momentum created in recent years to stop child labour, especially in its worst forms, to reflect on the progress made so far, and to pursue fresh efforts to achieve a future without child labour.

National and regional programmes have flourished under the ILO International Programme on the Elimination of Child Labour, which began with six participating countries in 1992 with a single donor government (Germany), and has expanded to include operations in 75 countries funded by 26 donors. In

2001, the ILO launched its first Time-Bound Programmes aimed at eliminating the worst forms of child labour in specific countries within 5 to 10 years. The first programmes are aimed at helping some 100,000 children in El Salva-dor, Nepal and Tanzania.

The report says partnerships between governments, employers' and workers' organisations, with other civil society organisations, and with the support of the international community, mean that real progress is being made in getting children out of work which is damaging them, and into school, in supporting them and their families to develop better, more secure livelihoods, and in preventing other children from being drawn into child labour.

'This foundation must be built upon, expanded and sustained,' Mr Somavia said. 'The effective abolition of child labour is one of the most urgent challenges of our time, and should be a universal goal.'

Notes

1 *A Future Without Child Labour: Global Report under the Follow-up to the ILO Declaration on Fundamental Principles and Rights at Work*, International Labour Conference, 90th Session, 2002, Report I (B). International Labour Office, Geneva, ISBN 92-2-112416-9.

2 See Art.3 (a) to (c), ILO Worst Forms of Child Labour Convention, 1999 (No. 182).

■ The above article first appeared in *World of Work*, No. 43, June 2002, a magazine produced by the International Labour Organization (ILO). Visit their web site at <u>www.ilo.org</u> for more information.

© 2003 *International Labour Organization (ILO)*

Early marriage

. . . is the marriage of children and adolescents below the age of 18

According to UNICEF's Innocenti Research Centre, the 'practice of marrying girls at a young age is most common in Sub-Saharan African and South Asia'. There are specific parts of West Africa and East Africa and of South Asia where marriages before puberty are not unusual. However, the Centre also notes that marriage shortly after puberty is common among those living traditional lifestyles in the Middle East, North Africa and other parts of Asia. Marriages of female adolescents between sixteen and eighteen are common in parts of Latin America and Eastern Europe.

Some are forced into this union, others are simply too young to make an informed decision. Consent is made by somebody else on the child's behalf. The child does not have the opportunity to exercise her right to choose. For this reason, early marriages are also referred to as forced marriages. In its most extreme form, forced marriages are the result of abductions. In Uganda, young girls are abducted and forced to marry senior leaders in the guerrilla movement known as the Lord's Resistance Army. The marriages are used as a reward and incentive for male soldiers.

Case study

In some countries, child marriages are bound to religious practices, but a thinly veiled form of child prostitution. In India young girls, known as Devadasi, are dedicated or married to a Hindu deity or temple in the hope that the gods will bestow blessings and good fortune upon the families. The Devadasi are expected to provide sexual services to the priests and members of the higher castes. Reportedly, many are eventually sold to urban brothels. Similar practices can be found in western Nepal where the girls are known as Deuki. The practice in India is now illegal.
(Source: *Questions and Answers about Commercial Sexual Exploitation of Children*. An information booklet by ECPAT International. 2001.)

There are a number of reasons why tradition of child marriages continues. Fear of HIV infection has encouraged men in many countries to seek younger 'partners'. Early marriages are one way to ensure that young girls are 'protected'. Families in rural Albania encourage their daughters to marry early to avoid the threat of kidnapping. In conflict-torn Somalia, families married their daughters to militia members in exchange for protection for the girl, as well as for themselves.

Where poverty is acute, early marriage is also seen as a strategy for economic survival. In Iraq, early marriages are on the increase in response to poverty inflicted by the economic sanctions that have been imposed on the country. In situations such as this, the risk of exploitation is great. A recent study of five poor villages in Egypt, for example, found that young girls were being married off to much older men from the oil-rich Middle Eastern countries via brokers.

Many girls who are forced to marry early suffer from prolonged domestic violence. Furthermore, early marriage is often linked to wife abandonment. This plungers young girls into extreme poverty and increases the risk of them entering, or being forced to enter, the commercial sex trade.

At times, the marriage was never intended to be a permanent union. Temporary marriages are possible via a short term marriage contact, known as Siqueh in Iran. Combined with a low legal age of marriage it is possible to circumvent the illegal act of child prostitution.

In Bangladesh, poverty-stricken parents are persuaded to part with their daughters through promises of marriage, or false marriages, which are used to lure the girls into prostitution abroad. Police in Cambodia say that hundreds, perhaps thousands of young women have been lured to Taiwan with promises of marriage to wealthy men, only to find themselves sold to a brothel owner.

■ The above information is from ECPAT's web site which can be found at www.ecpat.net

© ECPAT International

Sexual exploitation and the human rights of girls

Early marriage

Introduction

Marriage is usually greeted as a joyful occasion. It displays the union of two families and the creation of a new domestic unit to continue the hopes and values of the community. In reality, however, for girl children, the event often represents a serious abuse of human rights.

For the vast majority of girl children in the world, their basic human rights are overwhelmed and constrained by power structures that measure their worth in terms of their economic value or cost as commodity items. From birth they are treated less favourably than their brothers. The child mortality rates for girls are generally higher than for boys. Girls are worked harder, receive less nourishing food and immunisations and are less likely to receive medical care when ill. Girls receive less education than boys. If girls do attend school, they complete fewer grades than boys. Marriage, relentless hard work and child-bearing are an almost inevitable premature end to a girl's childhood and formal education. Status is determined by gender and in many countries female children occupy the lowest position.

Increasing urbanisation and globalisation have resulted in the crumbling of family structures and with this family ties and obligations. Poverty and commercialisation expose the most vulnerable individuals to exploitation and abuse whether of their labour or sexuality. There is evidence that in some parts of the world early marriage is on the increase. Parents may be forced by poverty to marry off their daughter in the hope of giving her a better life and of reducing the numbers draining their family's meagre resources. With the AIDS pandemic there is also an increasing demand for younger and younger girls to marry older men.

Family poverty

Poverty is one of the explanations for selling girls, sometimes because the family is in debt or because of the benefits of the sale. In August 2001, a Forum member was told about a ten-year-old girl in Zimbabwe who was reported in a local newspaper as having been sold to be a wife to a 40-year-old man in order for the family to obtain cash for food. She was sold for $2000 Zim. That worked out at US$7. This sum would perhaps have bought two sacks of maize. The previous wife of the man the child was to marry had died of AIDS.

Marriage, relentless hard work and child-bearing are an almost inevitable premature end to a girl's childhood and formal education

---

Although many countries have set a minimum legal age for marriage, the age for girls is usually set 2-3 years lower than it is for boys; at a local level the majority of marriages take place without reference to the national standard. In some regions, girls continue to be betrothed before or at birth. In others, girls will be sent to live with their husband's family years before puberty and although it is not expected that the marriage will be consummated immediately, available evidence would suggest that this is often not respected. In these circumstances, it is highly unlikely that the girl will have either the knowledge or the power of control over her reproductive capacity.

Early marriage consumes many years of a girl's adolescence, com-promising her schooling, life choices and future health. In these situations, girls are often condemned to lives of misery, servitude, sexual abuse and premature childbirth while they are still children themselves and, therefore, before they have even reached the internationally agreed age of consent.

In many countries around the world girls are given away, bought, sold or exchanged like other commodity items in the market-place in the name of marriage. This is accepted because it is a custom and because the arrangement will have been made as part of a wider framework of connections between or within social groups. However, in general, it is unlikely that as part of this process, the human rights of the girl concerned will have been considered.

The human rights of girls

Over the last five decades, various UN and other international legal conventions, charters, protocols and declarations concerned with the promotion of women's and children's rights have been ratified and signed up to by many, and in the case of the CRC, the majority of countries. Additional legislation aimed at the abolition of gender-based violence and the sexual exploitation of children is receiving high-level international support. It is increasingly being acknowledged that the needs and rights of girl children demand particular attention.

Alemtsehai
'When I was 10 my parents arranged for me to marry in the forest. They pretended it was just a party. But it was a wedding and they sent me away. My mother never told me I was going to be married. They came and took me by force. I cried but it didn't make any difference.'

The 1989 UN Convention on the Rights of the Child (CRC) defines childhood as lasting until an individual reaches the age of 18. Yet in most of the countries in Africa, Asia, Latin America and the Middle East, the majority of girls will have been married before this age. Although much of the CRC is relevant to child marriage, it does not specifically refer to it. In principle, the matter of child marriage and girls' rights is covered by the Vienna Declaration and Programme of Action, section B4 of which deals with the Rights of the Child. Paragraph B49 of the declaration 'urges States to repeal existing laws and regulations and remove customs and practices which discriminate against and cause harm to the girl child'.

In spite of international agreements to implement measures to protect children from slavery, discrimination and other forms of sexual abuse and exploitation, there appears to be little recognition that the same forms of abuse occur within the domestic setting of marriage. Although several countries have a minimum legal age for marriage, each year millions of girls will be sold or exchanged in marriage ceremonies by their families at ages below the legal age. Many will have barely reached the age of puberty and their bodies not yet fully grown to maturity.

The UN Convention on Consent to Marriage, Minimum Age for Marriage and Registration of Marriages (CCMMAMRM) was ratified in 1964; however in some cultures girls as young as nine or ten are married, in many cases to much older men. In its preamble, the CCMMAMRM recalls article 16 of the 1948 Universal Declaration of Human Rights (UNDHR) which specifically refers to: 'Men and women of full age' and states that 'marriage shall be entered into only with the free and full consent of the intending spouses'. Article 3 of the 1964 Convention requires that States register all marriages in an official register. However, precise statistics on early marriage are difficult to obtain, as, still, few marriages are formally registered.

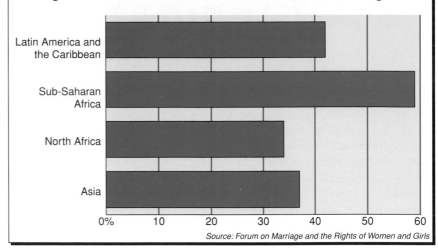

Proportion of women already married at 20

Precise statistics on early marriage are difficult to obtain, as, still, few marriages are formally registered. Accurate data do not exist, but the graph below gives an idea of the numbers of women married before the age of 20.

Source: Forum on Marriage and the Rights of Women and Girls

Early and forced marriages violate the human rights of girls by virtue of the fact that the fundamental basis of the marriage is often not based on the free and full consent of both parties. In addition, where the girl may have consented to the marriage on the basis of having reached the sexual age of consent, this may not equate to an age of immaturity with regard to marriage. The Platform for Action from the Fourth UN World Conference on Women spells out the human rights of women to: *'include their right to have control over and decide freely and responsibly on matters related to their sexuality, including sexual and reproductive health, free of coercion, discrimination, and violence. Equal relationships between women and men in matters of sexual relations and reproduction, including full respect for the integrity of the person, require mutual respect, consent and shared responsibility for sexual behaviour and its consequences.'* (1995, Beijing Platform for Action, para. no. 86).

Furthermore, there is usually a gulf between a country's international commitment on paper and its domestic action to ensure that these commitments are implemented in practice. It has been argued that once international instruments are applied in the domestic context, common law and practice will eventually fit. This is not proving to be the case. There is no clearer example of the mismatch between international human rights legislation and commitments and daily lives than in the impact on girls of early and forced marriage.

■ The Forum is a network of organisations mainly based in the UK with international affiliates, sharing a vision of marriage as a sphere in which women and girls have inalienable rights. Our shared commitment to social justice places central importance on the need to bring principles and rights which are accepted in the public sphere into effective operation in the private sphere, particularly in marriage.

As a Forum we are committed to the inalienability of the human rights of girls and women throughout their lives, which cannot be reduced or violated by marriage, and to the breaking down of barriers that impact adversely on their rights within marriage. We promote the rights of women and girls including social rights, reproductive and political right and the rights to full inheritance and to marry or not. Forum members work together, sharing information on models of good practice and carrying out joint advocacy activities for the greater realisation of these rights.

■ The above information is an extract from a report produced by the Forum on Marriage and the Rights of Women and Girls.

© *Forum on Marriage and the Rights of Women and Girls, Save the Children*

Child participation

Myth and reality

Myth: Child participation means choosing one child to represent children's perspectives and opinions in an adult forum.
Reality: Children are not a homogeneous group, and no one child can be expected to represent the interests of their peers of different ages, races, ethnicities and gender. Children need forums of their own in which they can build skills, identify their priorities, communicate in their own way and learn from their peers. In this way, children are better able to make their own choices as to who should represent their interests and in which ways they would like their viewpoints presented.

Myth: Child participation involves adults handing over all their power to children who are not ready to handle it.
Reality: Participation does not mean that adults simply surrender all decision-making power to children. The Convention on the Rights of the Child (CRC) is clear that children should be given more responsibility – according to their 'evolving capacities' as they develop. In many cases adults still make the final decision, based on the 'best interests' of the child – but with the

CRC in mind, it should be a decision informed by the views of the child. As children grow older, parents are to allow them more responsibility in making decisions that affect them – even those that may be controversial, such as custody matters following a divorce.

Myth: Children should be children, and not be forced to take on responsibilities that should be given to adults.
Reality: Children should certainly be allowed to be children, and to receive all the protection necessary to safeguard their healthy development. And no children should be forced to take on responsibilities for which they are not ready. But children's healthy development also depends upon being allowed to engage with the world, making more independent decisions and assuming more responsibility as they become more capable. Children who encounter barriers to their participation may become frustrated or even

apathetic; 18-year-olds without the experience of participation will be poorly equipped to deal with the responsibilities of democratic citizenship.

Myth: Child participation is merely a sham. A few children, usually from an elite group, are selected to speak to powerful adults who then proceed to ignore what the children have said while claiming credit for 'listening' to kids.
Reality: Children's participation, in many instances, has proven to be very effective. Rather than setting up an ineffectual system, it is up to all of us to devise meaningful forms of children's participation that benefit them and, in turn, society as a whole.

Myth: Child participation actually only involves adolescents, who are on the verge of adulthood anyway.
Reality: The public, political face of children's participation is more likely to be that of an adolescent than a 6-year-old, but it is essential to consult children of all ages about the issues that affect them. This means participation within schools and families, when decisions about

matters there are being discussed. At every age children are capable of more than they are routinely given credit for – and will usually rise to the challenges set before them if adults support their efforts.

Myth: No country in the world consults children on all the issues that affect them and no country is likely to do so soon.
Reality: That's partly true. However, all countries that have ratified the Convention on the Rights of the Child have committed themselves to ensuring participation rights for children, e.g., the rights to freely express their views on matters that affect them and to freedom of thought, conscience, religion, association and peaceful assembly. And almost every country can now show significant advances in setting systems and policies in place to allow children to exercise these rights.

Myth: Children may be consulted as a matter of form but their views never change anything.
Reality: Where children's views are sensitively solicited and sincerely understood, they often change a great deal: they may reveal things that adults would never have grasped independently, they can profoundly change policies or programmes and in some cases protect children from future harm. The consultation of even very young children can produce remarkable results. The problem is that such careful consultation of children remains rare.

Myth: Children's refusal to participate negates their rights.
Reality: Actually, resistance itself can be an important part of participation. Whether in the give and take of the home, in the refusal to accept punishment at school, or in one's attitude towards civic engagement in the community, resistance can signal a child's or adolescent's opinion about an issue or feeling about the terms of their involvement. Adults should recognise resistance as a form of communication and respond to it through understanding, dialogue and negotiation, rather than by trying to prevent it through force or persuasion. In no situation should children be forced to participate.

■ The above information is from UNICEF International's web site which can be found at www.unicef.org
© UNICEF

We are the world's children

Information from UNICEF

United Nations Children's Fund

The Special Session on Children, 8-10 May 2002, was an unprecedented meeting of the UN General Assembly dedicated to the children and adolescents of the world. It brought together government leaders and Heads of State, NGOs, children's advocates and young people themselves. Some 400 young delegates from all over the world gathered in New York for the event.

After three days of discussion and debate during the Children's Forum, an event preceding the United Nations' Special Session on Children, some 400 young people agreed on a statement to be presented to world leaders. Gabriela Azurduy Arrieta, 13, from Bolivia and Audrey Cheynut, 17, from Monaco were chosen by their peers to represent them. As the Special Session commenced on 8 May 2002, these two young delegates to the Forum stood before the General Assembly and delivered their message. On this historic occasion, for the first time ever, children formally addressed the UN General Assembly on behalf of children, giving voice to their vision for a better world.

In this world
We see respect for the rights of the child:
■ governments and adults having a real and effective commitment

For the first time ever, children formally addressed the UN General Assembly on behalf of children, giving voice to their vision for a better world

to the principle of children's rights and applying the Convention on the Rights of the Child to all children,
■ safe, secure and healthy environments for children in families, communities and nations.

We see an end to exploitation, abuse and violence:
■ laws that protect children from exploitation and abuse being implemented and respected by all,
■ centres and programmes that help to rebuild the lives of victimised children.

We see an end to war:
■ world leaders resolving conflict through peaceful dialogue instead of by using force,
■ child refugees and child victims of war protected in every way and having the same opportunities as all other children,
■ disarmament, elimination of the arms trade and an end to the use of child soldiers.

We see the provision of health care:

- affordable and accessible life-saving drugs and treatment for all children,
- strong and accountable partnerships established among all to promote better health for children.

We see the eradication of HIV/AIDS:

- educational systems that include HIV prevention programmes,
- free testing and counselling centres,
- information about HIV/AIDS freely available to the public,
- orphans of AIDS and children living with HIV/AIDS cared for and enjoying the same opportunities as all other children.

We see the protection of the environment:

- conservation and rescue of natural resources,
- awareness of the need to live in environments that are healthy and favourable to our development,
- accessible surroundings for children with special needs.

We see an end to the vicious cycle of poverty:

- anti-poverty committees that bring about transparency in expenditure and give attention to the needs of all children,
- cancellation of the debt that impedes progress for children.

We see the provision of education:

- equal opportunities and access to quality education that is free and compulsory,
- school environments in which children feel happy about learning,
- education for life that goes beyond the academic and includes lessons in understanding, human rights, peace, acceptance and active citizenship.

We see the active participation of children:

- raised awareness and respect among people of all ages about every child's right to full and

A world fit for us

We are the world's children.
We are the victims of exploitation and abuse.
We are street children.
We are the children of war.
We are the victims and orphans of HIV/AIDS.
We are denied good-quality education and health care.
We are victims of political, economic, cultural, religious and environmental discrimination.
We are children whose voices are not being heard: it is time we are taken into account.
We want a world fit for children, because a world fit for us is a world fit for everyone.

meaningful participation, in the spirit of the Convention on the Rights of the Child,

- children actively involved in decision-making at all levels and in planning, implementing, monitoring and evaluating all matters affecting the rights of the child.

We pledge an equal partnership in this fight for children's rights. And while we promise to support the actions you take on behalf of children, we also ask for your commitment and support in the actions we are taking – because the children of the world are misunderstood.

We are not the sources of problems; we are the resources that are needed to solve them.

We are not expenses; we are investments.

We are not just young people; we are people and citizens of this world.

Until others accept their responsibility to us, we will fight for our rights.

We have the will, the knowledge, the sensitivity and the dedication.

We promise that as adults we will defend children's rights with the same passion that we have now as children.

We promise to treat each other with dignity and respect.

We promise to be open and sensitive to our differences.

We are the children of the world, and despite our different backgrounds, we share a common reality.

We are united by our struggle to make the world a better place for all.

You call us the future, but we are also the present.

- The above information is from UNICEF International's web site which can be found at www.unicef.org

Human rights comes to life

Human Rights Act – an introduction

What is the Human Rights Act?

The Human Rights Act 1998 is a new law in full force from 2 October 2000. It gives further effect in the UK to the fundamental rights and freedoms in the European Convention on Human Rights (ECHR).

What does it do?

The new law does three simple things:

- It makes it unlawful for a public authority, like a government department, local authority or the police, to breach the Convention rights, unless an Act of Parliament meant it couldn't have acted differently
- It means that cases can be dealt with in a UK court or tribunal. Until now, anyone who felt that their rights under the Convention had been breached had to go to the European Court of Human Rights in Strasbourg
- It says that all UK legislation must be given a meaning that fits with the Convention rights, if that's possible. If a court says that's not possible it will be up to Parliament to decide what to do

What is the European Convention on Human Rights?

This is one of the earliest and most important treaties passed by the Council of Europe, a group of nations invited by Sir Winston Churchill to come together after the Second World War to stop such atrocities and acts of cruelty happening again.

The Council of Europe is quite separate from the European Union (EU). It has its own Court of Human Rights in Strasbourg. You are already able to go to the Strasbourg court to claim your rights under the ECHR. However, the ECHR has until now not been part of the UK's domestic law. So our courts have not normally been able to deal with claims.

Your convention rights

There are sixteen basic rights in the Human Rights Act, all taken from the European Convention on Human Rights. They don't only affect matters of life and death like freedom from torture and killing; they also affect your rights in everyday life: what you can say and do, your beliefs, your right to a fair trial and many other similar basic entitlements.

(Article 1 is introductory)

Article 2 – Right to life

You have the absolute right to have your life protected by law. There are only certain very limited circumstances where it is acceptable for the State to take away someone's life, e.g. if a police officer acts justifiably in self-defence.

Article 3 – Prohibition of torture

You have the absolute right not to be tortured or subjected to treatment or punishment which is inhuman or degrading.

Article 4 – Prohibition of slavery and forced labour

You have the absolute right not to be treated as a slave or forced to perform certain kinds of labour.

Article 5 – Right to liberty and security

You have the right not to be deprived of your liberty – 'arrested or detained'

– except in limited cases specified in the Article (e.g. where you are suspected or convicted of committing a crime) and where this is justified by a clear legal procedure.

Article 6 – Right to a fair trial

You have the right to a fair and public hearing within a reasonable period of time. This applies to both criminal charges against you, or in sorting out cases concerning your civil rights and obligations. Hearings must be by an independent and impartial tribunal established by law. It is possible to exclude the public from the hearing (though not the judgement) if that is necessary to protect things like national security or public order. If it is a criminal charge you are presumed innocent until proved guilty according to law and have certain guaranteed rights to defend yourself.

Article 7 – No punishment without law

You normally have the right not to be found guilty of an offence arising out of actions which at the time you committed them were not criminal. You are also protected against later increases in the possible sentence for an offence.

The rights in Articles 8 to 11 may be limited where that is necessary to achieve an important objective. The precise objectives in each Article which allow limitations vary, but they include things like protecting public health or safety, preventing crime, and protecting the rights of others.

Article 8 – Right to respect for private and family life

You have the right to respect for your private and family life, your home and your correspondence. This right can only be restricted in specified circumstances.

Article 9 – Freedom of thought, conscience and religion

You are free to hold a broad range of views, beliefs and thoughts, as well as religious faith. Limitations are permitted only in specified circumstances.

Article 10 – Freedom of expression

You have the right to hold opinions and express your views on your own or in a group. This applies even if they are unpopular or disturbing. This right can only be restricted in specified circumstances.

Article 11 – Freedom of assembly and association

You have the right to assemble with other people in a peaceful way. You also have the right to associate with other people, which can include the right to form a trade union. These rights may be restricted only in specified circumstances.

Article 12 – Right to marry

Men and women have the right to marry and start a family. The national law will still govern how and at what age this can take place.

(Article 13 is not included in the Human Rights Act)

Article 14 – Prohibition of discrimination

In the application of the Convention rights, you have the right not to be treated differently because of your race, religion, sex, political views or any other status, unless this can be justified objectively. Everyone must have equal access to Convention rights, whatever their status.

Article 1 of Protocol 1 – Protection of property

(a 'protocol' is a later addition to the Convention)

You have the right to the peaceful enjoyment of your possessions. Public authorities cannot usually interfere with things you own or the way you use them except in specified limited circumstances.

Article 2 of Protocol 1 – Right to education

You have the right not to be denied access to the educational system.

Article 3 of Protocol 1 – Right to free elections

Elections for members of the legislative body (e.g. Parliament) must be free and fair and take place by secret ballot. Some qualifications may be imposed on those that are eligible to vote (e.g. a minimum age).

Article 1 of Protocol 6 / Article 2 of Protocol 6 – Abolition of the death penalty

These provisions abolish the death penalty. There can be limited exceptions in times of war but only in accordance with clearly specified laws.

How does the Human Rights Act affect me?

Does the Human Rights Act change my rights?

No. But the Human Rights Act makes claiming your rights much quicker and easier. Instead of having to go to Strasbourg, you can now bring a case in a court in the UK.

Does the Human Rights Act affect the way government and public bodies behave?

Yes. The Human Rights Act says that all public authorities must pay proper attention to your rights when they are making decisions that affect you. Public authorities include Government Ministers, civil servants, your local authority or health authority, and also agencies like the police, the courts and private companies when carrying out public functions. That's nothing new – respecting rights and balancing rights and responsibilities have always been an important part of public service in this country. But the Human Rights Act makes sure that those in authority over you will have to check that they do not ride roughshod over your rights, even when they believe they are doing so for a good reason. They will have to be careful about the balance they are striking and think hard about how they can cause the least possible harm to individuals.

People who work for public authorities have been trained in the new law. And every time Government proposes a new law in Parlia-ment it has to make a statement under the Human Rights Act about how the new law fits in with the Convention rights.

Can I use the Human Rights Act against another private individual who infringes my rights?

Not directly. You cannot sue, or be sued by, another individual for breaking the Convention rights. But you may benefit indirectly because the Human Rights Act means all laws have to be given a meaning and effect which is as close as possible to the Convention rights. It's also a lot easier to insist on your rights if they are written down. You can point them out to the person who you think is ignoring them.

But what about responsibilities? Are my rights under the Act unlimited?

They are not. Most of the rights in the Human Rights Act have some boundaries to prevent them unfairly affecting the rights of others – or overriding the rights of the wider community. In a democratic society everyone has rights. Your rights come

first, but so do everyone else's. So we all have to accept some limits on our rights in order to make sure others are treated fairly.

For example, someone's right to liberty might have to be restricted if they have committed a crime. Freedom of speech cannot mean the freedom to shout 'Fire!' in a crowded hall, when there isn't one.

Will the Human Rights Act really change anything?

It should do. This is a type of higher law, affecting all other laws. The rights and their limitations are really a set of basic values. Respect for the rights and everything that goes with them should help change the way people think and behave and create an atmosphere in which decisions and policies are discussed and understood. How far the Human Rights Act will improve the quality of life for all in the UK depends on how far we all respect the values it enshrines.

What does the Human Rights Act mean for democracy?

Democracy is the only form of government which fits with the Convention rights. Tolerance and broad-mindedness are the bedrock of democracy – and the bedrock of the Convention rights. The Human Rights Act recognises the central place of Parliament in our democracy. It should encourage transparency and openness in Government because public authorities will use the language of the Convention rights to debate problems. Because that's a language we can all understand we will be better able to understand what's being said – and to join in.

Will the Human Rights Act please everyone?

Not all the time. There is bound to be argument over some decisions and clashes between rights. We won't all agree on subjects like measures about privacy, victims' rights or freedom of expression. The Human Rights Act may affect decisions on these things. Some people are bound to feel that the wrong answer is reached. But the Human Rights Act should ensure proper debate and that basic rights are respected in a balanced way.

What does the Human Rights Act mean for our courts and judges?

The Human Rights Act will help them protect individuals' Convention rights. And they will be able to check that the rights of the wider community are properly balanced. If individuals' rights have to be affected, the public authority will need to show that it is not using a sledgehammer to crack a nut. This is often referred to as 'proportionality': interfering with rights only so far as it is necessary in order to achieve a specific purpose set out in the Convention.

For example, there is a fundamental right to assembly – and a right to meet with others.

So if the police or public authorities are thinking of banning certain demonstrations or restricting marches to certain routes, they must not just impose a blanket ban. They must think carefully about what is proportionate so they don't go any further than necessary to guard against the risks to others which they reasonably anticipate. Every court in the land has been trained to help you when a public authority is acting against your rights.

So will the courts be able to overrule Parliament?

No. The Human Rights Act specifically says judges can't overrule Parliament. But the courts will be able to develop the law in line with the Convention rights. Judges have always been able to develop the law themselves. But the Human Rights

Act means they will operate within a democratic code of values, based on your Convention rights.

Does the Human Rights Act mean more court cases?

Not in the long run. Going to court is always a last resort. The Human Rights Act will help clarify rights and public authorities will soon understand how the courts are likely to interpret the law. In the early days people may try to use the new law to find out just how the balance will be struck between their rights and other people's rights. But judges have already made it clear that they will not want to waste time on arguments that have no merit.

For example, one of our fundamental rights is to marry if we are of marriageable age. In the UK the law sets this at 16. It would almost certainly be regarded as a time-waster to go to court to argue that you should be allowed to marry at a younger age. This is the sort of decision that every country is allowed to take for itself.

What about Scotland, Wales and Northern Ireland?

The Parliament in Westminster has power to pass any laws, no matter what the Convention says. The Assemblies in Wales and Northern Ireland and the Parliament in Scotland do not have this power. If they pass laws which don't fit with the Convention rights the courts will overrule them.

Something for everyone

On Human Rights Day, 10 December 2002, the British Institute of Human Rights (BIHR) launched its report *Something for Everyone*

The report looks at the effects of the Human Rights Act on disadvantaged communities, and the need for a human rights commission in the UK.

Supported by a grant from Comic Relief BIHR commissioned this report to assess the impact of the Human Rights Act (HRA) to date on disadvantaged groups. The report also looks at what further steps, including the creation of a Human Rights Commission, might be necessary if the potential of the Act is to be realised and a human rights culture is to take root.

The evidence from participants in the research across four sectors – children, older people, refugees and asylum-seekers, and disabled people – indicated that there is no serious attempt from either government or the voluntary sector to use the Human Rights Act to create a human rights culture that could in turn lead to systemic change in the provision of services by public authorities.

Candy Whittome, Co-Director of BIHR, said, 'This report, which is the first to look at the difference the HRA has made to the lives of vulnerable people, shows how urgently we need an independent body that can effectively promote and protect human rights. The government should seize the opportunity presented by the consultation into the single equality body project by creating an Equalities and Human Rights Commission.'

The project found overwhelming support for the establishment of a Human Rights Commission – or for a similar sort of body that could promote and protect human rights. Such a commission would meet the need that currently exists for good quality advice, guidance and training on the Act itself. As importantly it would also promote the principles that underlie the legislation in a way that everyone can understand.

'I think one thing is that people – the whole community – aren't aware of human rights as anything that's good for them. It needs some publicity, it needs somebody to take it forward: it needs the dissemination of knowledge so that people realise what it's good for – and it's good for them. I think it's really important for them to know that they can use human rights. You know, it's something for everyone; it's for the good of the people.'

(Cheryl Monteith, Refugee Support Centre.)

This support is driven by the report's other main findings.

- Awareness of the Act has not in general spread outside the legal field. The absence of a human rights culture leaves a void. The Act is considered to be the domain of lawyers and legal policy staff: very few organisations used it systematically in their parliamentary lobbying or in their work with civil servants for example. Without more attention paid to the promotion of the Human Rights Act and the principles which lie behind it in a way that makes it accessible to lay people the vicious circle of unresponsive public services which lead to legal challenges cannot be broken.

- Individual members of staff in public services have no understanding of their responsibilities under the Human Rights Act. The lack of any ongoing concerted promotional strategy for the Act means that staff who provide public services – particu-

> *Awareness of the Act has not in general spread outside the legal field. The absence of a human rights culture leaves a void*

HUMAN RIGHTS DAY

larly front-line staff – fail to understand what the Act is, the rights that it contains, and the responsibilities that they have to uphold it. A Commission could have a key role, working in partnership with regulatory, training, and industry bodies, to demonstrate that the Act is not simply about legal challenges; rather, it gives all staff in the public sector a responsibility to promote and uphold human rights.

- There is little or no understanding of the Act as a useful framework for public service providers within which problems can be solved and risks assessed, and within which the needs of individuals in the provision of services can be considered. This may be particularly useful for areas where the rights of one individual may need to be balanced against the rights of others, perhaps leading to restrictions on rights which can be justified using the Act's concept of proportionality. Such a framework could enable public service workers to make difficult decisions about allocation of resources, or protection of vulnerable children or adults, with more confidence.

- There is no single authoritative source of advice and information that could help to shape the development of a human rights culture in the absence of a Human Rights Commission.

The report concludes that there is an urgent need for evidence-based research to enable public policy makers as well as equalities and human rights practitioners to understand more about the gaps in protection for people's rights that will exist if a single equality body does not include a human rights dimension.

Notes

Something for Everyone was commissioned by the British Institute of Human Rights. It was funded by Comic Relief and researched and written by Jenny Watson. The British Institute of Human Rights is a charity (registration no. 262121) based in the Law School of King's College University which has for over thirty years been educating people about the importance of human rights. Today it has a significant voice advocating for the human rights of the most disadvantaged and vulnerable com-

munities across the UK and striving to make human rights relevant for all.

For more information see our website at www.bihr.org

Comic Relief is seriously committed to helping end poverty and social injustice in the UK and Africa. Since its launch in 1985, Comic Relief has raised over £250 million to help some of the poorest and most vulnerable people in the UK and Africa to help themselves. For every pound that Comic Relief gets from the public, a pound will go directly to projects helping hundreds of thousands of people change their lives. For more information on Comic Relief visit : www.comicrelief.com

■ The above information is from the British Institute of Human Rights's web site: www.bihr.org

© British Institute of Human Rights (BIHR)

Universal Declaration of Human Rights

Preamble

Whereas recognition of the inherent dignity and of the equal and inalienable rights of all members of the human family is the foundation of freedom, justice and peace in the world,

Whereas disregard and contempt for human rights have resulted in barbarous acts which have outraged the conscience of mankind, and the advent of a world in which human beings shall enjoy freedom of speech and belief and freedom from fear and want has been proclaimed as the highest aspiration of the common people,

Whereas it is essential, if man is not to be compelled to have recourse, as a last resort, to rebellion against tyranny and oppression, that human rights should be protected by the rule of law,

Whereas it is essential to promote the development of friendly relations between nations,

Whereas the peoples of the United Nations have in the Charter reaffirmed their faith in fundamental human rights, in the dignity and worth of the human person and in

the equal rights of men and women and have determined to promote social progress and better standards of life in larger freedom,

Whereas Member States have pledged themselves to achieve, in cooperation with the United Nations, the promotion of universal respect for and observance of human rights and fundamental freedoms,

Whereas a common understanding of these rights and freedoms is of the greatest importance for the full realisation of this pledge,
Now, therefore,
The General Assembly,
Proclaims this Universal Declaration

of Human Rights as a common standard of achievement for all peoples and all nations, to the end that every individual and every organ of society, keeping this Declaration constantly in mind, shall strive by teaching and education to promote respect for these rights and freedoms and by progressive measures, national and international, to secure their universal and effective recognition and observance, both among the peoples of Member States themselves and among the peoples of territories under their jurisdiction.

Article 1

All human beings are born free and equal in dignity and rights. They are endowed with reason and conscience and should act towards one another in a spirit of brotherhood.

Article 2

Everyone is entitled to all the rights and freedoms set forth in this Declaration, without distinction of any kind, such as race, colour, sex, language, religion, political or other opinion, national or social origin, property, birth or other status.

Furthermore, no distinction shall be made on the basis of the political, jurisdictional or international status of the country or territory to which a person belongs, whether it be independent, trust, non-self-governing or under any other limitation of sovereignty.

Article 3
Everyone has the right to life, liberty and security of person.

Article 4
No one shall be held in slavery or servitude; slavery and the slave trade shall be prohibited in all their forms.

Article 5
No one shall be subjected to torture or to cruel, inhuman or degrading treatment or punishment.

Article 6
Everyone has the right to recognition everywhere as a person before the law.

Article 7
All are equal before the law and are entitled without any discrimination to equal protection of the law. All are entitled to equal protection against any discrimination in violation of this Declaration and against any incitement to such discrimination.

Article 8
Everyone has the right to an effective remedy by the competent national tribunals for acts violating the fundamental rights granted him by the constitution or by law.

Article 9
No one shall be subjected to arbitrary arrest, detention or exile.

Article 10
Everyone is entitled in full equality to a fair and public hearing by an independent and impartial tribunal, in the determination of his rights and obligations and of any criminal charge against him.

Article 11
1 Everyone charged with a penal offence has the right to be presumed innocent until proved

guilty according to law in a public trial at which he has had all the guarantees necessary for his defence.
2 No one shall be held guilty of any penal offence on account of any act or omission which did not constitute a penal offence, under national or international law, at the time when it was committed. Nor shall a heavier penalty be imposed than the one that was applicable at the time the penal offence was committed.

Article 12
No one shall be subjected to arbitrary interference with his privacy, family, home or correspondence, nor to attacks upon his honour and reputation. Everyone has the right to the protection of the law against such interference or attacks.

Article 13
1 Everyone has the right to freedom of movement and residence within the borders of each State.
2 Everyone has the right to leave any country, including his own, and to return to his country.

Article 14
1 Everyone has the right to seek and to enjoy in other countries asylum from persecution.
2 This right may not be invoked in

All human beings are born free and equal in dignity and rights. They are endowed with reason and conscience and should act towards one another in a spirit of brotherhood

the case of prosecutions genuinely arising from non-political crimes or from acts contrary to the purposes and principles of the United Nations.

Article 15
1 Everyone has the right to a nationality.
2 No one shall be arbitrarily deprived of his nationality nor denied the right to change his nationality.

Article 16
1 Men and women of full age, without any limitation due to race, nationality or religion, have the right to marry and to found a family. They are entitled to equal rights as to marriage, during marriage and at its dissolution.
2 Marriage shall be entered into only with the free and full consent of the intending spouses.
3 The family is the natural and fundamental group unit of society and is entitled to protection by society and the State.

Article 17
1 Everyone has the right to own property alone as well as in association with others.
2 No one shall be arbitrarily deprived of his property.

Article 18
Everyone has the right to freedom of thought, conscience and religion; this right includes freedom to change his religion or belief, and freedom, either alone or in community with others and in public or private, to manifest his religion or belief in teaching, practice, worship and observance.

Article 19
Everyone has the right to freedom of opinion and expression; this right includes freedom to hold opinions without interference and to seek, receive and impart information and ideas through any media and regardless of frontiers.

Article 20
1 Everyone has the right to freedom of peaceful assembly and association.
2 No one may be compelled to belong to an association.

Article 21

1 Everyone has the right to take part in the government of his country, directly or through freely chosen representatives.
2 Everyone has the right to equal access to public service in his country.
3 The will of the people shall be the basis of the authority of government; this will shall be expressed in periodic and genuine elections which shall be by universal and equal suffrage and shall be held by secret vote or by equivalent free voting procedures.

Article 22

Everyone, as a member of society, has the right to social security and is entitled to realisation, through national effort and international co-operation and in accordance with the organisation and resources of each State, of the economic, social and cultural rights indispensable for his dignity and the free development of his personality.

Article 23

1 Everyone has the right to work, to free choice of employment, to just and favourable conditions of work and to protection against unemployment.
2 Everyone, without any discrimination, has the right to equal pay for equal work.
3 Everyone who works has the right to just and favourable remuneration ensuring for himself and his family an existence worthy of human dignity, and supplemented, if necessary, by other means of social protection.
4 Everyone has the right to form and to join trade unions for the protection of his interests.

Article 24

Everyone has the right to rest and leisure, including reasonable limitation of working hours and periodic holidays with pay.

Article 25

1 Everyone has the right to a standard of living adequate for the health and well-being of himself and of his family, including food, clothing, housing

and medical care and necessary social services, and the right to security in the event of unemployment, sickness, disability, widowhood, old age or other lack of livelihood in circumstances beyond his control.
2 Motherhood and childhood are entitled to special care and assistance. All children, whether born in or out of wedlock, shall enjoy the same social protection.

Article 26

1 Everyone has the right to education. Education shall be free, at least in the elementary and fundamental stages. Elementary education shall be compulsory. Technical and professional education shall be made generally available and higher education shall be equally accessible to all on the basis of merit.
2 Education shall be directed to the full development of the human personality and to the strengthening of respect for human rights and fundamental freedoms. It shall promote understanding, tolerance and friendship among all nations, racial or religious groups, and shall further the activities of the United Nations for the maintenance of peace.
3 Parents have a prior right to choose the kind of education that shall be given to their children.

Article 27

1 Everyone has the right freely to participate in the cultural life of the community, to enjoy the arts and to share in scientific advancement and its benefits.

2 Everyone has the right to the protection of the moral and material interests resulting from any scientific, literary or artistic production of which he is the author.

Article 28

Everyone is entitled to a social and international order in which the rights and freedoms set forth in this Declaration can be fully realised.

Article 29

1 Everyone has duties to the community in which alone the free and full development of his personality is possible.
2 In the exercise of his rights and freedoms, everyone shall be subject only to such limitations as are determined by law solely for the purpose of securing due recognition and respect for the rights and freedoms of others and of meeting the just requirements of morality, public order and the general welfare in a democratic society.
3 These rights and freedoms may in no case be exercised contrary to the purposes and principles of the United Nations.

Article 30

Nothing in this Declaration may be interpreted as implying for any State, group or person any right to engage in any activity or to perform any act aimed at the destruction of any of the rights and freedoms set forth herein.

© Office of the United Nations High Commissioner for Human Rights, Geneva, Switzerland

New survey documents global repression

Information from Human Rights Watch

(Washington, DC, January 14, 2003) – Global support for the war on terrorism is diminishing partly because the United States too often neglects human rights in its conduct of the war, Human Rights Watch said today in releasing its World Report 2003.

Terrorists violate basic human rights principles because they target civilians. But the United States undermines those principles when it overlooks human rights abuses by anti-terror allies such as Pakistan, China, Saudi Arabia and Afghan warlords, Human Rights Watch said in its annual survey of human rights around the world.

The 558-page *Human Rights Watch World Report 2003* covers human rights in 58 countries in 2002. It identifies positive trends such as the formal end to wars in Angola, Sudan, and Sierra Leone, as well as peace talks in Sri Lanka. But negative developments included the outbreak of serious communal violence in Gujarat, India, and the continued killing of civilians in wars from Colombia to Chechnya, from the Democratic Republic of Congo to the Israeli-Palestinian conflict. Meanwhile, governments continued highly repressive policies in Burma, China, Cuba, Iran, Iraq, Liberia and Vietnam.

Washington has so much power today that when it flouts human rights standards, it damages the human rights cause worldwide

---

'The United States is far from the world's worst human rights abuser,' said Kenneth Roth, executive director of Human Rights Watch. 'But Washington has so much power today that when it flouts human rights standards, it damages the human rights cause worldwide.'

Human Rights Watch said the Bush administration seemed to recognise the connections between repression and terrorism in its National Security Strategy, and had taken some steps to promote human rights in countries directly involved in the struggle against terrorism, such as Egypt and Uzbekistan. The United States has also tried to advance human rights in places where the war was not implicated, including Burma, Belarus and Zimbabwe. Yet the US government's engagement on human rights has been compromised by its unwillingness to confront a number of crucial partners, and its refusal to be bound by standards it preaches to others.

'To fight terrorism, you need the support of people in countries where the terrorists live,' said Roth. 'Cosying up to oppressive govern-

ments is hardly a way to build those alliances.'

For example, the United States is generating popular resentment in Pakistan by uncritically backing General Pervez Musharraf, who took power in a 1999 coup.

'He's still tight with us on the war against terror, and that's what I appreciate,' US President George Bush said about Musharraf, who last year pushed through constitutional amendments to extend his presidential term by five years and recently strengthened a draconian anti-terror decree.

In China, the Bush administration has downplayed the repression of Muslims in the north-west Xinjiang province, which the Chinese government justifies as an anti-terrorist measure. Saudi Arabia, with its highly repressive government, is an important regional player and the US government rarely challenges it on human rights.

The Bush administration is seeking to reinvigorate ties to the Indonesian military, despite the lack of accountability for its serious human rights abuses and the military's support for militia groups that foster instability. The United States has also been reluctant to expand the international peace-keeping forces that could help bring stability to Afghanistan, relying instead on abusive warlords who are inhibiting the human rights progress made possible by the fall of the Taliban.

In addition, Washington has ignored human rights standards in its own treatment of terrorist suspects. It has refused to apply the Geneva Conventions to prisoners of war from Afghanistan, and has misused the designation of 'enemy combatant' to apply to criminal

suspects on US soil. The Bush administration has also abused immigration laws to deny criminal suspects their rights.

In 2002, the US government actively tried to undermine important human rights initiatives such as the International Criminal Court, a new international inspection regime to prevent torture, and a United Nations resolution that the war on terrorism should be fought in a manner consistent with human rights.

The war against terror has provided an excuse for other Western countries to slacken their support for human rights. European leaders virtually abandoned efforts to pressure Russia, an anti-terror ally, to end its abusive conduct of the war in Chechnya.

Human Rights Watch does not take a position on the possible war in Iraq, and believes that its most important contribution to reducing the civilian suffering that war entails is to monitor and promote the compliance by all warring parties with international humanitarian law.

Roth noted that the more US government officials cite Saddam Hussein's human rights record as one reason to topple him, the greater their obligation to minimise the potentially serious human rights consequences of any war in Iraq. The

United States should take all feasible measures to protect Iraqi civilians from acts of revenge by Saddam Hussein, including the possible use of weapons of mass destruction. At minimum, it should make clear that anyone who directs or commits atrocities will be prosecuted, not just a handful of senior Iraqi officials.

The war against terror has provided an excuse for other Western countries to slacken their support for human rights

---

The United States should ensure that its local allies in any Iraq war do not engage in revenge killings or reprisals against civilians. And the Bush administration should also put pressure on Iraq's neighbours, such as Turkey, Jordan and Iran, to keep their borders open to refugees.

■ Human Rights Watch is an international monitoring group based in New York, with offices around the world. It does not accept funding from any government.

© 2003, *Human Rights Watch*

Women's rights

Information from Human Rights Watch

'After the school break, my mom asked me if I wanted to go back to school. I said no. I didn't want to go. All the people who I thought were my friends had turned against me. And they [the rapists] were still there [at school].'
W.H., age 13, gang-raped by boys from her school, quoted in Human Rights Watch report *Scared at School: Sexual Violence against Girls in South African Schools.*

Millions of women throughout the world live in conditions of abject deprivation of, and attacks against, their fundamental human rights for no other reason than that they are women.

Combatants and their sympathisers in conflicts, such as those in Sierra Leone, Kosovo, the Democratic Republic of Congo, Afghanistan, and Rwanda, have raped women as a weapon of war with near complete impunity. Men in Pakistan, South Africa, Peru, Russia, and Uzbekistan beat women in the home at astounding rates, while these governments alternatively refuse to intervene to protect women and punish their batterers or do so haphazardly and in ways that make women feel culpable for the violence. As a direct result of inequalities found in their countries of origin, women from Ukraine, Moldova, Nigeria, the Dominican Republic, Burma, and Thailand are bought and sold, trafficked to work in forced prostitution, with insufficient government attention to protect their rights and punish the traffickers. In Guatemala, South Africa, and Mexico, women's ability to enter and remain in the work force is obstructed by private employers who use women's reproductive status to exclude them from work and by discriminatory employment laws or discriminatory enforcement of the law. In the US, students discriminate against and attack girls in school who are lesbian, bi-sexual, or transgendered, or do not conform to male standards of female behaviour.

Women in Morocco, Jordan, Kuwait, and Saudi Arabia face government-sponsored discrimination that renders them unequal before the law – including discriminatory family codes that take away women's legal authority and place it in the hands of male family members – and restricts women's participation in public life.

Abuses against women are relentless, systematic, and widely tolerated, if not explicitly condoned. Violence and discrimination against women are global social epidemics, notwithstanding the very real progress of the international women's human rights movement in identifying, raising awareness about, and challenging impunity for women's human rights violations.

We live in a world in which women do not have basic control over what happens to their bodies. Millions of women and girls are forced to marry and have sex with men they do not desire. Women are unable to depend on the government to protect them from physical violence in the home, with sometimes fatal consequences, including increased risk of HIV/AIDS infection. Women in state custody face sexual assault by their jailers. Women are punished for having sex outside of marriage or with a person of their choosing (rather than of their family's choosing). Husbands and other male family members obstruct or dictate women's access to reproductive health care. Doctors and government officials disproportionately target women from disadvantaged or marginalised communities for coercive family planning policies.

Our duty as activists is to expose and denounce as human rights violations those practices and policies that silence and subordinate women. We reject any law, culture, or religion in which women are systematically discriminated against, excluded from political participation and public life, segregated in their daily lives, raped in armed conflict, beaten in their homes, denied equal divorce or inheritance rights, killed for having sex, forced to marry, assaulted for not conforming to gender norms, and sold into forced labour. Arguments that sustain and excuse these human rights abuses – those of cultural norms, 'appropriate' rights for women, or western imperialism – barely disguise their true meaning: that women's lives matter less than men's. Cultural relativism, which argues that there are no universal human rights and that rights are culture-specific and culturally determined, is still a formidable and corrosive challenge to women's rights to equality and dignity in all facets of their lives.

The Women's Rights Division of Human Rights Watch fights against the dehumanisation and marginalisation of women. We promote women's equal rights and human dignity. The realisation of women's rights is a global struggle based on universal human rights and the rule of law. It requires all of us to unite in solidarity to end traditions, practices, and laws that harm women. It is a fight for freedom to be fully and completely human and equal without apology or permission. Ultimately, the struggle for women's human rights must be about making women's lives matter everywhere all the time. In practice, this means taking action to stop discrimination and violence against women.

■ The above information is from Human Rights Watch's web site which can be found at www.hrw.org
© 2003, *Human Rights Watch*

Slavery in the 21st century

An estimated 27 million people are enslaved around the world.[1] Forced to work through violence or the threat of it, they are under the complete control of their 'employers'. They are treated as property and sometimes bought and sold

Bonded labour

Kinds of work
Farming, brick-making, carpet-weaving, domestic labour, stone quarrying, sex work . . .

Terms
Hard work in return for a loan, either of money or resources. Interest repayments may be hugely inflated. Workers may be tricked into taking the loans or may have had no other option. Contracts are rare.

Location
Traditionally India, Pakistan and Nepal. But has expanded to global proportions. Includes children trafficked between West African countries, men forced to work on Brazilian estates, and Eastern European women bonded into Western Europe's sex industry.

Prohibitions
The UN Supplementary Convention on the Abolition of Slavery, the Slave Trade, and Institutions and Practices Similar to Slavery (1956) prohibits bonded labour at an international level. Many countries have national legislation.

Trafficking

Kinds of work
Farming, child camel jockeys, domestic labour, fishing, mail-order brides, market stall labour, small repair shop work, restaurant labour, sex industry . . .

Terms
Transported far from their homes, people lured by the promise of a better life are forced through violence, threats and deception to work in conditions of slavery.

Location
The trade in human beings affects every continent and most countries.

Job description

Sex
Male or female

Age
Any age; from 4 until death

Characteristics
Poor and vulnerable; minorities where applicable

Hours
Up to 20 a day, sometimes more

Days per week
Up to 7; 365 days a year

Holidays
None

Sick leave
None

Health and safety provision
None

Pay
Below the minimum wage, often nothing

Accommodation
Basic; often provided in lieu of pay or deducted from it

Prohibitions
The UN Protocol to Prevent, Suppress and Punish Trafficking in Persons, Especially Women and Children (2000). Some countries, such as Benin, have national legislation.

Child slaves

Kinds of work
Farming, camel jockeys, domestic labour, drug trafficking, fireworks manufacturing, fishing, brick-making, carpet-weaving, sex work, stone quarrying, soldiers . . .

Terms
Often more abject than for adult slaves as children are more vulnerable to abuse. Children taken out of familiar surroundings are completely at the mercy of the slavekeepers.

Location
Extensive evidence of child slaves in the Gulf States, South Asia, West and Central Africa. Sexual exploitation of children is found throughout the world.

Prohibitions
Under international law anyone under 18 is a child. The UN Convention on the Rights of the Child (1989) and the International Labour Organization's (ILO) Worst Forms of Child Labour Convention (1999) provide legal prohibition. Most countries also have domestic legislation.

Forced labour

Kinds of work
Construction, maintenance of roads, rails and bridges, farming, domestic labour . . .

Terms
When an individual is forced to work against their will, under threat of violence or other punishment, with restrictions on their freedom and a degree of ownership is exerted over them.

Location
Burma, China, Sudan and elsewhere.

Prohibitions
The ILO's forced labour conventions (numbers 29 and 105) carry strong

prohibitions. And the 1998 ILO Declaration on Fundamental Principles and Rights at Work obliges all member states to promote core conventions, including the forced labour conventions, regardless of whether they have ratified them or not.

Marriage as slavery

Early marriage
Girls as young as 10 married without a choice and unable to give informed consent are forced into lives of domestic servitude and often physical violence.

Forced marriage
Women in parts of rural China and the Central Asian Republics are abducted and forced to marry men from neighbouring villages.

Servile marriage
Girls are pledged to priests in Ghana, Togo, Benin and Nigeria to atone for an offence committed by a family member. They are domestic and sexual slaves. Women from the old slave caste in Niger may still be obliged to become second wives to a man from the owner caste and act as servants for the first wife.

Girls as young as 10 are married without a choice and unable to give informed consent are forced into lives of domestic servitude and often physical violence

---

Prohibitions
There are numerous, including in the *Universal Declaration of Human Rights* (1948) and the *UN Convention on the Rights of the Child* (1999).

Traditional slavery

Kinds of work
Farming, domestic labour, haulage, anything demanded by the slave-keepers.

Terms
In Sudan, women and children from villages in the South are abducted by

Percentage of women aged 25-29, married before age 18[2]	
Latin America	
Guatemala	39%
Dominican Republic	38%
Paraguay	24%
Asia	
Bangladesh	81%
Nepal	68%
Pakistan	37%
Indonesia	34%
Sub-Saharan Africa	
Niger	77%
Mali	70%
Burkina Faso	62%
Mozambique	57%
Malawi	55%
Côte d'Ivoire	44%
Cameroon	43%
Benin	40%
Middle East	
Yemen	64%
Egypt	30%

pro-Government militia and sold to households in the North. In Mauritania and Niger nomadic and semi-nomadic tribes have slave castes. Even among slaves who have managed to become free and earn money, a tribute must often be paid to their family's former master who also maintains inheritance rights over any property the free slave may have accrued.

Location
Mauritania, Niger and Sudan.

Prohibitions
Proscribed by the UN under the Slavery, Servitude, Forced Labour and Similar Institutions and Practices Convention (1926), the Universal Declaration of Human Rights (1948) and the Supplementary Convention on the Abolition of Slavery, the Slave Trade, and Institutions and Practices Similar to Slavery (1956).

References
1 All information, unless otherwise noted, from Anti-Slavery International. The facts about slavery are complex and difficult to measure – this is not an exhaustive account of existing slavery, nor does it cover all international laws that can be used to combat it. It's an introduction to the scale of this human-rights abuse.
2 Population Council, as cited in Early Marriage: Child Spouses, *Innocenti Digest* Number 7, March 2001, UNICEF.

■ The above information is from the *New Internationalist*'s web site which can be found at <u>www.newint.org</u>
© *New Internationalist*

Privacy and human rights

Information from a report published by Privacy International

Overview

Privacy is a fundamental human right. It underpins human dignity and other values such as freedom of association and freedom of speech. It has become one of the most important human rights of the modern age.

Privacy is recognised around the world in diverse regions and cultures. It is protected in the Universal Declaration of Human Rights, the International Covenant on Civil and Political Rights, and in many other international and regional human rights treaties. Nearly every country in the world includes a right of privacy in its constitution. At a minimum, these provisions include rights of inviolability of the home and secrecy of communications. Most recently written constitutions include specific rights to access and control one's personal information. In many of the countries where privacy is not explicitly recognised in the constitution, the courts have found that right in other provisions. In many countries, international agreements that recognise privacy rights such as the International Covenant on Civil and Political Rights or the European Convention on Human Rights have been adopted into law.

Defining privacy

Of all the human rights in the international catalogue, privacy is perhaps the most difficult to define.[1] Definitions of privacy vary widely according to context and environment. In many countries, the concept has been fused with data protection, which interprets privacy in terms of management of personal information.

Outside this rather strict context, privacy protection is frequently seen as a way of drawing the line at how far society can intrude into a person's affairs.[2] The lack of a single definition should not imply that the issue lacks importance. As one writer

observed, 'in one sense, all human rights are aspects of the right to privacy'.[3]

Some viewpoints on privacy:
In the 1890s, future United States Supreme Court Justice Louis Brandeis articulated a concept of privacy that urged that it was the individual's 'right to be left alone'. Brandeis argued that privacy was the most cherished of freedoms in a democracy, and he was concerned that it should be reflected in the Constitution.[4]

Robert Ellis Smith, editor of the *Privacy Journal*, defined privacy as 'the desire by each of us for physical space where we can be free of interruption, intrusion, embarrassment, or accountability and the attempt to control the time and manner of disclosures of personal information about ourselves'.[5]

According to Edward Bloustein, privacy is an interest of the human personality. It protects the inviolate personality, the individual's independence, dignity and integrity.[6]

According to Ruth Gavison, there are three elements in privacy: secrecy, anonymity and solitude. It is a state which can be lost, whether through the choice of the person in that state or through the action of another person.[7]

The Calcutt Committee in the United Kingdom said that, 'nowhere have we found a wholly satisfactory statutory definition of privacy'. But the committee was satisfied that it would be possible to define it legally and adopted this definition in its first report on privacy:
The right of the individual to be protected against intrusion into his personal life or affairs, or those of his family, by direct physical means or by publication of information.[8]

The Preamble to the Australian Privacy Charter provides that, 'A free and democratic society requires respect for the autonomy of individuals, and limits on the power of both state and private organisations to intrude on that autonomy...Privacy is a key value which underpins human dignity and other key values such as freedom of association and freedom of speech. Privacy is a basic human right and the reasonable expectation of every person.'[9]

Aspects of privacy

Privacy can be divided into the following separate but related concepts:
Information privacy, which involves the establishment of rules governing the collection and handling of personal data such as credit information, and medical and government

records. It is also known as 'data protection';

Bodily privacy, which concerns the protection of people's physical selves against invasive procedures such as genetic tests, drug testing and cavity searches;

Privacy of communications, which covers the security and privacy of mail, telephones, e-mail and other forms of communication; and

Territorial privacy, which concerns the setting of limits on intrusion into the domestic and other environments such as the workplace or public space. This includes searches, video surveillance and ID checks.

References

1 James Michael, *Privacy and Human Rights* 1 (UNESCO 1994).
2 Simon Davies, *Big Brother: Britain's Web of Surveillance and the New Technological Order* 23 (Pan 1996).
3 Volio, Fernando, 'Legal personality, privacy and the family' in Henkin (ed), *The International Bill of Rights* (Columbia University Press 1981).
4 Samuel Warren and Louis Brandeis, 'The Right to Privacy,' 4 *Harvard Law Review* 193-220 (1890).
5 Robert Ellis Smith, *Ben Franklin's Web Site* 6 (Sheridan Books 2000).
6 'Privacy as an Aspect of Human Dignity,' 39 *New York University Law Review* 971 (1964).
7 'Privacy and the Limits of Law,' 89 *Yale Law Journal* 421, 428 (1980).
8 Report of the Committee on Privacy and Related Matters, Chairman David Calcutt QC, 1990, Cmnd. 1102, London: HMSO, page 7.
9 'The Australian Privacy Charter,' published by the Australian Privacy Charter Group, Law School, University of New South Wales, Sydney 1994.

■ The above information is from the report *Privacy and Human Rights 2002*, produced by EPIC and Privacy International. For more information visit www.privacyinternational.org

Protection of privacy

UK singled out for criticism over protection of privacy. By Stuart Millar

Britain has one of the worst records in the developed world for protecting the privacy of its citizens, according to international research to be published tomorrow.

The survey of privacy conditions in 50 countries, carried out by Privacy International and the US-based Electronic Privacy Information Centre, singles out the UK for criticism over a series of law enforcement measures which the authors say have undermined civil liberties, especially since the September 11 terror attacks on the US last year.

The report concludes: 'There is, at some levels, a strong public recognition and defence of privacy . . . On the other hand, crime and public order laws passed in recent years have placed substantial limitations on numerous rights, including freedom of assembly, privacy, freedom of movement, the right of silence, and freedom of speech.'

In particular, the report highlights moves to allow law enforcement and other public bodies to demand access to telephone and internet records without obtaining a judicial or executive warrant. The anti-terror legislation rushed through parliament last autumn included provisions which will require communications service providers to keep their customers' records for longer periods so that the data are available to the authorities.

Britain has also been a key player behind the scenes in pushing data surveillance measures through at EU level.

Simon Davies, director of Privacy International, an independent watchdog, accused ministers of a 'systematic attack' on the right to privacy by introducing laws permitting mass surveillance.

'The UK demonstrates a pathology of antagonism toward privacy,' he said. 'The rate of growth of video surveillance, communications surveillance and information collection has exceeded the growth rate in such countries as Singapore and Israel.'

Mr Davies said legal protections over privacy had been 'weakened at a fundamental level' by government. 'The UK Data Protection Act is almost useless in limiting the growth of surveillance,' he added.

The report will be launched at a conference at the London School of Economics examining the impact on privacy of September 11. The researchers discovered an almost universal shift in the balance towards more surveillance and less privacy since September 11.

The report states: 'Among all of these measures, it is possible to identify a number of trends, including: increased communications surveillance and search and seizure powers; weakening of data protection regimes; increased data sharing; and increased profiling and identification. While none of the above trends are necessarily new, the novelty is the speed in which these policies gained acceptance and, in many cases, became law.'

While most countries in the developed world have laws intended to limit intrusions on privacy, the report found that in many cases these have been rendered redundant by the determination of governments to know more about their citizens.

Last night, the Home Office said that while some powers introduced under anti-terror and other laws infringed privacy, safeguards were in place to ensure the correct balance between civil liberties and security. 'September 11 meant that the nature and level of threat we faced was different and specific, and targeted measures were necessary to ensure that was addressed,' a spokeswoman said.

Secrets and lies

Freedom of information

What does freedom of information mean?

Freedom of information simply means the right to know. A Freedom of Information Act gives people the right to see information that is being held on them by public or other bodies, as well as information about the way they are governed, and about the natural and commercial environment in which they live.

The principle behind freedom of information is that there should be a public right to have access to information, unless there are real and specified reasons for secrecy e.g. national security. Supporters of freedom of information say that in a democratic society, unnecessary secrecy undermines the accountability of Government. It deprives people of access to the facts and undermines their ability to make informed decisions.

The present situation

Many politicians, and organisations, including Charter88, have been arguing for some time that we should have a Freedom of Information Act, but until recently there was no general and legally enforceable right to access to officially held information in this country. We only had a limited right to freedom of information in specific areas such as our own medical records. This meant we had no way of finding out how decisions were being made in many key areas such as housing, education and the environment,

The Labour Party has had a commitment to introduce a Freedom of Information Act in every election manifesto since 1974. The 1997 manifesto said:

'Unnecessary secrecy in government leads to arrogance in government and defective policy decisions . . . We are pledged to a Freedom of Information Act, leading to more open government.'

The Freedom of Information Bill was introduced and had its First Reading in the House of Commons on 18 November 1999. Five back-bench revolts during the Commons Report Stage forced the Government to make concessions to increase the powers of the Information Commissioner and restrict the use of the veto. The bill was introduced in the House of Lords in April 2000 and became law on 1 December 2000.

Implementation of the Act will start in April 2002 eventually covering information held by central government, local Government, the police, the health service, education and then all other public bodies.

Freedom of information in Scotland

From July 1999 the Scottish Executive introduced a non-statutory Code of Practice on Access to Scottish Executive Information (available on their website, www.scotland.gov.uk). This was based closely on the UK Code of Practice.

Freedom of information in Wales

In March 2000, the new First Secretary, Rhodri Morgan, started to publish minutes of Welsh Cabinet meetings six weeks after they were held. The Assembly has also issued a consultation paper on a new Freedom of Information Code of Practice in Wales.

Past problems

Some of the more controversial examples which illustrate the lack of freedom of information in this country include:

The principle behind freedom of information is that there should be a public right to have access to information

---

1. The 'Arms to Iraq' scandal

This was highlighted in 1992 when it was discovered that a British company had been sending arms to Iraq in breach of Government guidelines. Because the UK was at war in the Gulf, the directors of the company were charged with serious offences and would have faced prison sentences if they were convicted. When the matter came to Court, the Government refused to reveal information that it had known about these sales, which would have provided the men with a defence. It was only after an extensive inquiry that it was found out that members of the Government had allowed the sales to happen, without reporting to Parliament. This meant that the men concerned were not guilty of the offence they had been charged with, and the Government had tried to deliberately withhold the information that showed they were not guilty.

Would the Government have allowed these sales to happen if the public had been able to find out about it? Would those men have gone to prison if the Government had succeeded in withholding the information they needed for their defence?

2. The BSE crisis

In Britain a large number of British cows contracted a mystery illness that attacked their central nervous system. The Government reassured the public for a long time that there was no danger of people contracting the human form of the disease, through eating beef. However, in 1996 the Government did reveal that scientists had doubts about the safety of eating beef and the European Union stepped in to impose a world-wide ban on the export and import of British beef as a result. This ban was not lifted until the year 2000.

Should the public have had access to this information, so that they could have made up their own minds?

The limits on freedom of information

However, there are sometimes good reasons for keeping some information secret, for example:

1. National security

It may be important, especially in times of war, for Governments to keep information secret, to stop it falling into the wrong hands. For example, in the Gulf War, if the positioning of UK soldiers had been freely available, it would have endangered their lives.

2. Personal privacy

There may be subjects that are not so relevant to the public. For example should we have a right to know about the sexuality of public figures?

These examples illustrate exceptions to the principle of freedom of information and show that we need to debate such examples and work out where the public interest lies.

Freedom of information in other countries

Many other countries such as the United States, Australia, Canada, France, Sweden, and New Zealand have laws dealing with freedom of information. Sweden has had a Freedom of Information law for over 200 years!

After a Freedom of Information law was passed in Canada, it was discovered that almost half of Canadian hospitals were reusing medical equipment intended to be used only once. At least 20 deaths

were caused by this practice in one year alone.

What effects could the Freedom of Information Act have?

Opponents of the Freedom of Information Act say that it will only be used by journalists and pressure groups. They claim that it will be time-consuming and expensive to administer and that disputes will clog up the courts.

Supporters of freedom of information say that the point of the legislation is to improve access to information about matters that concern all of us. If Government decisions are exposed to more scrutiny, then expensive mistakes might be avoided. There is evidence of this from countries with existing Freedom of Information laws. It could lead to a culture of more open Government and a more transparent and thorough decision-making process.

Also, it is not always the case that such information is controversial. Sometimes it is simply inaccurate. A legal right of access to personal information about us could simply provide us with an opportunity to correct inaccuracies.

Finally, it is claimed that the Freedom of Information Act should not lead to a large number of court cases as it will be enforced by a Commissioner and tribunal.

In fact many organisations campaigning for freedom of information, including the Campaign for Freedom of Information and Charter88, have been disappointed by this Act. These organisations believe that the Government's original proposals for freedom of information have been watered down and the amount of information which will not be covered at all by the Act is larger than originally suggested.

However, the Campaign for Freedom of Information has also said that the Act will improve our rights as individuals to see personal files held on us. It will also help provide greater openness in local government, quangos, contractors and other bodies not previously covered by the open government codes.

It seems that there is a consensus amongst those who support freedom of information, that this legislation is a step in the right direction but that it still needs fundamental improvement if it is to be really effective in practice.

■ The above information is from Citizen21's web site which can be found at www.citizen21.org.uk

© Charter 88

KEY FACTS

- The United Nations Convention on the Rights of the Child was drawn up in 1989 and gives children and young people under 18 their own special set of rights. (p. 1)

- Children's rights are a set of entitlements for all children, of whatever age and background. Most children's rights supporters use the UN Convention on the Rights of the Child (UNCRC) as their guide to children's rights. (p. 6)

- The Children and Young People's Unit has a special responsibility to prepare reports for the Committee on the Rights on the Child on how well the UK is implementing the UN Convention on the Rights of the Child (UNCRC). (p. 7)

- The British public overwhelmingly support the rights of donor-conceived children to have a statutory right to know the identity of their biological parents. (p. 8)

- In 1991 the United Kingdom (UK) Government ratified the United Nations Convention on the Rights of the Child. Every government in the world apart from the USA and Somalia has ratified the Convention. (p. 9)

- Children's Rights Commissioners are national watchdogs for children and young people. They are not part of the Government. They monitor, protect and promote all the rights of the Convention for children. (p. 10)

- The Children's Commissioner for Wales was set up two years ago, and children in Scotland and Northern Ireland will soon have their own commissioners. (p. 10)

- The Children Act 1989 does not require parents or others with parental responsibility to consult their children or to take their views into account in making decisions about their upbringing. (p. 11)

- Young people under the age of 18 do not have an absolute right to refuse consent to medical treatment. Refusal to give consent in cases concerning serious mental health or life-threatening situations can be overridden if their parents – or if they are in care, the local authority – disagree with their decision. (p. 12)

- A MORI survey for the NSPCC in February 2002 found that, provided parents were not prosecuted for 'trivial smacks', a majority (58 per cent) of people in England and Wales support changing the law to give children protection from being hit. (p. 13)

- In 1998, the European Court of Human Rights ruled that UK law does not protect children adequately. (p. 13)

- Children are protected from being hit by law in Germany, Finland, Sweden, Denmark, Austria, Norway, Croatia, Cyprus, Latvia and Israel. The most recent country to ban physical punishment was Germany in 2000 and the first was Sweden in 1979. (p. 13)

- Children are the only people who do not have legal protection against all levels of violence. (p. 14)

- Studies show that over 90% of children have been smacked, spanked or beaten. (p. 14)

- Sometimes as young as six years old, children are forced to work under extremely difficult conditions, often as bonded labourers or in forced prostitution. (p. 15)

- One in every six children aged 5 to 17 – or 246 million children – are involved in child labour. (p. 16)

- One in every eight children in the world – some 179 million children aged 5 to 17 – are still exposed to the worst forms of child labour, which endanger their physical, mental or moral well-being. (p. 16)

- An estimated 27 million people are enslaved around the world. Forced to work through violence or the threat of it, they are under the complete control of their 'employers'. They are treated as property and sometimes bought and sold. (p. 34)

- Early marriage – girls as young as 10 married without a choice and unable to give informed consent are forced into lives of domestic servitude and often physical violence. (p. 35)

- Privacy is a fundamental human right. It underpins human dignity and other values such as freedom of association and freedom of speech. It has become one of the most important human rights of the modern age. (p. 36)

- Britain has one of the worst records in the developed world for protecting the privacy of its citizens, according to international research. (p. 37)

- A Freedom of Information Act gives people the right to see information that is being held on them by public or other bodies, as well as information about the way they are governed, and about the natural and commercial environment in which they live. (p. 38)

You might like to contact the following organisations for further information. Due to the increasing cost of postage, many organisations cannot respond to enquiries unless they receive a stamped, addressed envelope.

Barnardo's
Tanners Lane, Barkingside
Ilford, Essex, IG6 1QG
Tel: 020 8550 8822
Fax: 020 8551 6870
E-mail: media.team@barnardos.org.uk
Web site: www.barnardos.org.uk
Works with over 47,000 children, young people and their families in more than 300 projects across the county.

British Institute of Human Rights (BIHR)
King's College London
8th Floor, 75-79 York Road
London, SE1 7AW
Tel: 020 7401 2712
Fax: 020 7401 2695
E-mail: admin@bihr.org
Web site: www.bihr.org
Has for over thirty years been educating people about the importance of human rights.

Charter 88– Citizen 21
18a Victoria Park Square
London, E2 9PB
Tel: 020 8880 6088
Fax: 020 7684 3889
E-mail: citizen21@charter88.org.uk
Web site: www.charter88.org.uk and www.citizen21.org.uk
An independent campaign for a modern and fair democracy.

Children's Rights Alliance for England (CRAE)
94 White Lion Street
London, N1 9PF
Tel: 020 7278 8222
Fax: 020 7278 9552
E-mail: info@crights.org.uk
Web site: www.crights.org.uk
An alliance of over 180 organisations committed to promoting children's human rights.

The Children's Society
Edward Rudolf House
Margery Street
London, WC1X 0JL
Tel: 020 7841 4400
Fax: 020 7841 4500
E-mail: information@the-childrens-society.org.uk
Web site:
www.childrenssociety.org.uk
Concentrates on tackling the root causes of the problems children and young people face.

Forum on Marriage and the Rights of Women and Girls
c/o Policy and Practice Unit, Save the Children UK
17 Grove Lane
London, SE5 8RD
Tel: 020 7703 5400
Fax: 020 7793 7610
E-mail: enquiries@scfuk.org.uk
Web site:
www.savethechildren.org.uk
The forum is a network of organisations mainly based in the UK with international affiliates, sharing a vision of marriage as a sphere in which women and girls have inalienable rights.

Human Rights Watch
33 Islington High Street
London, N1 9LH
Tel: 020 7713 1995
Fax: 020 7713 1800
E-mail: hrwuk@hrw.org
Web site: www.hrw.org
Dedicated to protecting the human rights of people around the world.

International Labour Office (ILO)
Millbank Tower, 21-24 Mill Bank
London, SW1P 4QP
Tel: 020 7828 6401
Fax: 020 7233 5925
E-mail: london@ilo.org
Web site: www.ilo.org
The UN agency with global responsibility for work, employment and labour market issues.

Liberty
21 Tabard Street
London, SE1 4LA
Tel: 020 7403 3888
Fax: 020 7407 5354
E-mail: info@liberty-human-rights.org.uk
Web site: www.liberty-human-rights.org.uk
Works to protect civil liberties and promote human rights, within the UK.

NSPCC – National Society for the Prevention of Cruelty to Children
Westdon House, 42 Curtain Road
London, EC2A 3NH
Tel: 020 7825 2500
Fax: 020 7825 2525
E-mail: info@nspcc.org.uk
Web site: www.nspcc.org.uk
Has a network of Child Protection Teams and projects to protect children from abuse.

The Office of the High Commissioner for Human Rights (UNHCR-UNOG)
8-14 Avenue de la Paix
1211 Geneva 10, Switzerland
Tel: + 41 22 917 9000
E-mail: udhr@ohchr.org
Web site: www.ohchr.org

Privacy International
2nd Floor, Lancaster House
33 Islington High Street
London N1 9LH, UK
Tel: 07947 778247
E-mail: privacyint@privacy.org
Web site:
www.privacyinternational.org
A human rights group formed in 1990 as a watchdog on surveillance by governments and corporations.

Save the Children
17 Grove Lane
Camberwell
London, SE5 8RD
Tel: 020 7703 5400
Fax: 020 7703 2278
E-mail: enquiries@scfuk.org.uk
Web site:
www.savethechildren.org.uk
The leading UK charity working to create a better world for children.

UNICEF
Africa House, 64-78 Kingsway
London, WC2B 6NB
Tel: 0207 405 5592
Fax: 0207 405 2332
E-mail: info@unicef.org.uk
Web site: www.unicef.org.uk
A global champion for children's rights which makes a lasting difference by working with communities and governments.

INDEX

ACKNOWLEDGEMENTS

The publisher is grateful for permission to reproduce the following material.

While every care has been taken to trace and acknowledge copyright, the publisher tenders its apology for any accidental infringement or where copyright has proved untraceable. The publisher would be pleased to come to a suitable arrangement in any such case with the rightful owner.

Chapter One: Young People's Rights

What's all this about rights?, © Save the Children, *Children lecture MPs on their human rights*, © Telegraph Group Limited, London 2003, *Know your rights*, © UNICEF, *FAQs about children's rights*, © The Children's Rights Alliance for England (CRAE), *Birthrights*, © The Children's Society, *Right Here Right Now*, © The Children's Rights Alliance for England (CRAE), *Parental responsibility and children's rights*, © Liberty, *Physical punishment in the home*, © NSPCC 2002, *Children are unbeatable!*, © Barnardo's 2002, , *Children's rights*, © Human Rights Watch, *Child labour remains 'massive problem'*, © International Labour Organization (ILO), *Early marriage*, © ECPAT International, *Sexual exploitation and the human rights of girls*, © Forum on Marriage and the Rights of Women and Girls, *Child participation*, © UNICEF, *We are the world's children*, © UNICEF.

Chapter Two: Human and Civil Rights

Human rights comes to life, © Crown copyright is reproduced with the permission of Her Majesty's Stationery Office, *Something for everyone*, © British Institute of Human Rights (BIHR), *Universal Declaration of Human Rights*, © Office of the United Nations High Commissioner for Human Rights, Geneva, Switzerland, *New survey documents global repression*, © Human Rights Watch, *Women's rights*, © Human Rights Watch, *Slavery in the 21st century*, © New Internationalist, *Privacy and human rights*, © EPIC and Privacy International, *Protection of privacy*, © Guardian Newspapers Limited 2002, *Secrets and lies*, © Charter 88.

Photographs and illustrations:

Pages 1, 13, 23, 36: Pumpkin House; pages 3, 6, 11, 15, 21, 26, 31, 32, 35, 39: Simon Kneebone; pages 5, 10, 18, 30: Bev Aisbett.

Craig Donnellan
Cambridge
May, 2003